First World War
and Army of Occupation
War Diary
France, Belgium and Germany

56 DIVISION
Headquarters, Branches and Services
General Staff
1 January 1917 - 28 February 1917

WO95/2933/1

The Naval & Military Press Ltd
www.nmarchive.com
Published in association with The National Archives

Published by

The Naval & Military Press Ltd

Unit 10 Ridgewood Industrial Park,

Uckfield, East Sussex,

TN22 5QE England

Tel: +44 (0) 1825 749494

www.naval-military-press.com

www.nmarchive.com

This diary has been reprinted in facsimile from the original. Any imperfections are inevitably reproduced and the quality may fall short of modern type and cartographic standards.

© Crown Copyright
Images reproduced by permission of The National Archives, London, England, 2015.

Contents

Document type	Place/Title	Date From	Date To
Heading	GS 56th Division Janry 1917		
Heading	GS XI Corps. Dec 1915		
Heading	War Diary of "G" 56th Division From 1st Jany 1917 To 31st Jany 1917 (Volume XII)		
War Diary	Lagorgue	01/01/1917	31/01/1917
Operation(al) Order(s)	56th Divisional Order No. 66. Appendix I.	31/01/1917	31/01/1917
Map	Appendix I. Posts		
Operation(al) Order(s)	56th Divisional Order No. 63. Appendix I.	29/12/1916	29/12/1916
Operation(al) Order(s)	56th Divisional Order No. 64. Appendix I	10/01/1917	10/01/1917
Miscellaneous	Amendment to 56th Div. Order No. 64. Appendix I.	11/01/1916	11/01/1916
Operation(al) Order(s)	56th Divisional Order No. 65. Appendix I	22/01/1917	22/01/1917
Miscellaneous	Location Table For Infantry Brigades Appendix II		
Miscellaneous	56th Divisional Tactical Progress Report No. 66 from 6.0 a.m. 31st December to 8.0 a.m. 1st January 1917. Appendix III	01/01/1917	01/01/1917
Miscellaneous	56th Divisional Tactical Progress Report No. 67 from 8.0 a.m. 1st January to 8.0 a.m. 2nd January 1917.	02/01/1917	02/01/1917
Miscellaneous	56th Divisional Tactical Progress Report No. 68 from 8.0 a.m. 2nd January to 8.0 a.m. 3rd January 1917.		
Miscellaneous	56th Divisional Tactical Progress Report 69 from 8.0 a.m. 3rd January to 8.0 a.m. 4th January 1917.	04/01/1917	04/01/1917
Miscellaneous	56th Divisional Tactical Progress Report, No. 70 from 8.0 a.m. 4th January to 8.0. a.m. 5th January, 1917.	05/01/1917	05/01/1917
Miscellaneous	56th Divisional Tactical Progress Report No. 71 from 8.0 a.m. 5th January to 8.0 a.m. 6th January 1917.	06/01/1917	06/01/1917
Miscellaneous	56th Divisional Tactical Progress Report No. 72 from 8.0 a.m. 6th January to 8.0 a.m. January 7th 1917.	07/01/1917	07/01/1917
Miscellaneous	56th Divisional Tactical Progress Report No. 73 from 8.0 a.m. 7th January to 8.0 a.m. 8th January 1917.	08/01/1917	08/01/1917
Miscellaneous	56th Divisional Tactical Progress Report No. 74 from 8.0 a.m. January 8th to 8.0 a.m. January 9th 1917.	09/01/1917	09/01/1917
Miscellaneous	56th Divisional Tactical Progress Report No. 75 from 8.0 a.m. 9th January, to 8.0 a.m. 10th January 1917.	10/01/1917	10/01/1917
Miscellaneous	56th Divisional Tactical Progress Report No. 76. from 8.0 a.m. 10th January to 8.0 a.m. 11th January, 1917.	11/01/1917	11/01/1917
Miscellaneous	56th Divisional Tactical Progress Report No. 77 from 8.0 a.m. 11th January to 8.0 a.m. 12th January 1917.	12/01/1917	12/01/1917
Miscellaneous	56th Division Tactical Progress Report No. 78 from 8.0 a.m. January 12th to 8.0 a.m. January 13th 1917.	13/01/1917	13/01/1917
Miscellaneous	56th Divisional Tactical Progress Report No. 79. from 8.0 a.m. 13th Jany. to 8.0 a.m., 14th January, 1917.	14/01/1917	14/01/1917
Miscellaneous	56th Divisional Tactical Progress Report No. 80. from 8.0 a.m. 14th January to 8.0 a.m. 15th January, 1917.	15/01/1917	15/01/1917
Miscellaneous	56th Divisional Tactical Progress Report No. 81 from 8.0 a.m. 15th January to 8.0 a.m. 16th January 1917	16/01/1917	16/01/1917
Miscellaneous	56th Divisional Tactical Progress Report No. 82 from 8.0 a.m. 16th January to 8.0 a.m. 17th January 1917	17/01/1917	17/01/1917
Miscellaneous	56th Divisional Tactical Progress Report No. 83 from 8.0 a.m. 17th January 1917 to 8.0 a.m. 18th Jany. 1917.	18/01/1917	18/01/1917

Miscellaneous	56th Divisional Tactical Progress Report No. 84 from 8.0 a.m. 18th January to 8.0 a.m. 19th January 1917.	19/01/1917	19/01/1917
Miscellaneous	56th Divisional Tactical Progress Report No. 86 from 8.0 a.m. 19th January to 8.0 a.m. 20th January 1917	20/01/1917	20/01/1917
Miscellaneous	56th Divisional Tactical Progress Report No. 87 from 8.0 a.m. 21st January to 8.0 a.m. 21st January 1917	21/01/1917	21/01/1917
Miscellaneous	56th Divisional Tactical Progress Report No. 88 from 8.0 a.m. 21st January to 8.0 a.m. 22nd January 1917	22/01/1917	22/01/1917
Miscellaneous	56th Divisional Tactical Progress Report No. 89 from 8.0 a.m. 22nd January to 8.0 a.m. 23rd January 1917	23/01/1917	23/01/1917
Miscellaneous	56th Divisional Tactical Progress Report No. 90 from 8.0 a.m. 23rd January to 8.0 a.m. 24th January 1917	24/01/1917	24/01/1917
Miscellaneous	56th Divisional Tactical Progress Report No. 91 from 8.0 a.m. 24th January to 8.0 a.m. 25th January 1917	25/01/1917	25/01/1917
Miscellaneous	56th Divisional Tactical Progress Report No. 92 from 8.0 a.m. 25th January to 8.0 a.m. 26th January 1917	26/01/1917	26/01/1917
Miscellaneous	56th Divisional Tactical Progress Report No. 93 from 8.0 a.m. 26th January to 8.0 a.m. 27th January 1917	27/01/1917	27/01/1917
Miscellaneous	56th Divisional Tactical Progress Report No. 94 from 8.0 a.m. 27th to 8.0 a.m. 28th January, 1917.	28/01/1917	28/01/1917
Miscellaneous	56th Divisional Tactical Progress Report No. 95 from 8.0 a.m. 28th January to 8.0 a.m. 29th January 1917.	29/01/1917	29/01/1917
Miscellaneous	56th Divisional Tactical Progress Report No. 96 from 8.0 a.m. 29th January to 8.0 a.m. 30th January 1917	30/01/1917	30/01/1917
Miscellaneous	56th Divisional Tactical Progress Report No. 97 from 8.0 a.m. 30th January to 8.0 a.m. 31st January 1917. Appendix III	31/01/1917	31/01/1917
Heading	Feb 1917		
Miscellaneous	A the national archives		
Heading	War Diary of "G" Branch 56th Division from 1st February to 28th February 1917 (Volume XIII)		
War Diary	La Gorgue	01/02/1917	28/02/1917
Operation(al) Order(s)	Warning Order 56th Divisional Order No. 67.	22/02/1917	22/02/1917
Miscellaneous	Move of 49th Division.		
Miscellaneous	Move of 56th Division.		
Miscellaneous	Amendment To Warning Order No. 67	23/02/1917	23/02/1917
Operation(al) Order(s)	56th Divisional Order No. 68	23/02/1917	23/02/1917
Map	Posts & Boundaries To Accompany Div. O.O. 68.		
Miscellaneous	56th Division S.G. 414/6	24/02/1917	24/02/1917
Miscellaneous	56th Divn. S.G. 415/7	25/02/1917	25/02/1917
Miscellaneous	Reference 56th Divn. S.G. 415/7 of 25.2.17, Dump at M.27.d.7.3. for "common to Left & Centre Brigades" read "Right & Centre Brigades"	25/02/1917	25/02/1917
Operation(al) Order(s)	56th Division Order No. 69	25/02/1917	25/02/1917
Miscellaneous	Location Table For Infantry Brigades		
Miscellaneous			
Miscellaneous	Divisional Headquarters-Willeman.		
Miscellaneous	Amendments & Additions to 56th Div. Order No. 69, dated 25.2.17	28/02/1917	28/02/1917
Miscellaneous	Location Table for Infantry Brigade.		
Miscellaneous	Boubers Artillery Area. Divisional Artillery H.Q.-Boubers-Sur-Canche.		
Miscellaneous	St. Michel Grouches and Anvin Artillery Areas.		
Miscellaneous	56th Division March & Relief Table to accompany 56th Div. Order No. 69		

Miscellaneous	49th Division March & Relief Table to accompany 56th Div. Order No. 69
Miscellaneous	Pernes Area Divisional Headquarters-Pernes.
Miscellaneous	The following constitute Brigade Groups.

56th Division
Janry 1917

Index..................

SUBJECT.

No.	Contents.	Date.

G.S.

XI Corps.

Dec 1915

CONFIDENTIAL

Vol 12

War Diary
of
"G" 56th Division

From 1st Jan 1917
To 31st Jan 1917
(Volume XII)

Army Form C. 2118.

WAR DIARY
or
INTELLIGENCE SUMMARY.
(Erase heading not required.)

Instructions regarding War Diaries and Intelligence Summaries are contained in F. S. Regs., Part II. and the Staff Manual respectively. Title pages will be prepared in manuscript.

Place	Date	Hour	Summary of Events and Information	Remarks and references to Appendices
LAGORGUE	1st Jan		Enemy lines were entered at many points during the night & found deserted on each occasion. At 1 pm the enemy commenced an organized bombardment of the whole of our front & line was kept up + our rear on back areas till dusk. Little damage was done, but some 1/15 casualties were caused, mainly amongst working parties – Our artillery retaliated vigorously during this period and the Renvies cooperated.	
	2nd Jan		April night. The plumed craters of No mans land and the Battle Line opposite the left section is becoming worse. We carried on an organized bombardment of enemy lines & communications during the day.) by OC carried out in relief.	Appendix II
	3rd Jan		During the night the enemy lines were entered in two places, where they held up who has reached, opposite the left section. It is noted that the enemy from line from M 30 c 28 to N 14.06 has been abandoned. – The relief of 169 Bde by 167 Bde in the night section was completed by 6 pm as per Divisional APPENDIX I	O.O. N63
	4th Jan		Against period – That measures received from Corps to take steps to establish posts in the abandoned enemy front line	
	5th Jan		Nothing to report during the 24 hours.	

Army Form C. 2118.

WAR DIARY
or
INTELLIGENCE SUMMARY.
(Erase heading not required.)

Instructions regarding War Diaries and Intelligence Summaries are contained in F.S. Regs., Part II. and the Staff Manual respectively. Title pages will be prepared in manuscript.

Place	Date	Hour	Summary of Events and Information	Remarks and references to Appendices
LA GORGUE	Jan 6th		In addition to the usual patrolling Lewis gun, Stokes mortars were turned onto the enemy front line and 40 rounds were fired from three at the LOZENGE. The whole of the SUGAR LOAF was patrolled and reported unoccupied and abandoned. This extends the further of our support lines which it has been established have been abandoned by the enemy, beyond the northern-hand end boundary. During the day we carried out decisive shoots on MIN DU PIETRE and what seems to be increasing the probable enemy fronts, the Riffle section. The enemy were quiet all day. Our patrols were active during the night and brought back many answers from the hostile lines, several made inspections at points of danger. W/Q2. were instructed to lay RE to take steps to establish posts in the abandoned enemy front line.	
	Jan 7th		During the day we carried out shoots on enemy working near DISTILLERY and NEST with good results.	
	Jan 8.		Our patrols again examined the portions of the German trenches which have been abandoned. A German patrol fired on one of our patrols who were repairing the enemy wire near TRIVELET. The enemy were quiet all day. 167 Bde carried out an initial relief	Appendix II

Army Form C. 2118.

WAR DIARY
or
INTELLIGENCE SUMMARY.
(*Erase heading not required.*)

Place	Date	Hour	Summary of Events and Information	Remarks and references to Appendices
LA GORGUE	Jan 9		In accordance with instructions 167 Bde issued orders that four posts should be established in the abandoned German front line. Each post to consist of 1 Lewis Gun team + three selected privates under an offr Sergeant, with an officer to each pair of posts. To be reinforced at night. Our patrols reconnoitred the German line + selected sites at N.14.a.75.25. N.13.d.95.15. N.13.d.8.6 + N.13.c.62.02. 168 Bde carried out an informal relief.	Appendix II
	Jan 10		The four posts were duly established during the night. That at N.14.a.75.25 met until 6.15 am owing its reoccupation by a strong hostile patrol. Enemy quiet all day.	
	Jan 11		Last night our offrs patrol ambushed a German patrol killed two the remainder taking to flight. Quiet day. Sleet falling during the afternoon.	
	Jan 12		Corps Conference held at xCorps H.Qs: G.O.C. G.S.I. AA+QMG CRA + CRE of this Division were present. Last night our patrols selected two more posts in the German line. These were established tonight at N.19.a.45.80 and N.19.a.35.30. Making six posts held by us in the German trenches. There was a slight howitzer encounter at the latter post during the night, otherwise quiet.	

WAR DIARY
or
INTELLIGENCE SUMMARY.
(Erase heading not required.)

Army Form C. 2118.

Place	Date	Hour	Summary of Events and Information	Remarks and references to Appendices
La Gorgue	Jan 13		Quiet day. Just after dusk our post at N.19.a.3.3. was rushed by a large party of the enemy, one of our men is missing. The enemy remained in occupation all night & worked hard all night. So the post could not be re-established though several attempts were made. Further South at M.24 d 5.1. one of our patrols penetrated 150 yds into the enemy trenches but found no one.	
	Jan 14		About 9.30 am the enemy captured BERTHA Post N.13 d 97.74. Four of the garrison were killed & 3 taken prisoner & 5 escaped. The mist was very thick. A subsequent patrol found that the enemy had evacuated the post so it was re-established about 12 noon. The relief of 167 Bde Infantry Bde by 169 Bde was carried out in accordance with Divisional Operation Order No. 64 and Amendment thereto. Brigadier-General G.H.B. Freeth C.M.G.,D.S.O. assumed command of the division in place of Brigadier General P.S. Coke C.M.G.	Appendix I Appendix II
	Jan 15		Quiet day. Snow and frost. 168 Bde carried out an internal relief.	
	Jan 16		Quiet day	
	Jan 17		The two posts we hold in the German front line are being rapidly consolidated. The water is still very high. A German patrol which attempted to reach our line at M.24.c.2. was fired on by a Lewis gun a man being seen to fall.	

WAR DIARY
or
INTELLIGENCE SUMMARY.
(Erase heading not required.)

Army Form C. 2118.

Place	Date	Hour	Summary of Events and Information	Remarks and references to Appendices
La Gorgue	Jan 18	3.30 am	A small party attempted to raid a portion of the German front line at M30 a 5.6. but found the wire had been repaired & the trench thickly manned. A bombing fight ensued in which casualties were inflicted on the enemy. A German barrage placed on our C.T. caught this party going back. A hostile party which attempted to reach BERTHA Post was driven off. Our artillery responding very quickly. Later in the day our artillery bombarded the enemy position opposite with good effect, but of no patrol parties the Germans subsequently sent at M30 b 55 90 but found no signs of the enemy. Weather very bad, some snow.	
	Jan 19		Quiet day. Hostile artillery shelled ENFIELD Post the guns replied vigorously, one of our patrols entered the German line at M30 a 40 15 a new point but could not find any enemy. 169 Bde carried out an internal relief.	Appendix II
	Jan 20		Much artillery activity on both sides. At about 6.45 pm the enemy made some of a violent bombardment round BERTHA Post. An immediate counter attack failed under his m.g. fire. A further counter attack under cover of our artillery + T.M.s was organised at 5.20 am the post was reoccupied. Quiet day save for slight shelling of our posts. 168 Bde carried out an internal relief.	Appendix V
	Jan 21			

Army Form C. 2118.

WAR DIARY
or
INTELLIGENCE SUMMARY.
(Erase heading not required.)

Instructions regarding War Diaries and Intelligence Summaries are contained in F. S. Regs., Part II. and the Staff Manual respectively. Title pages will be prepared in manuscript.

Place	Date	Hour	Summary of Events and Information	Remarks and references to Appendices.
La Gorgue	Jan 22		Quiet day. Some hostile shelling of our posts	
		6.30 pm	An enemy patrol which attempted to reach IRMA Post was driven off	
		6.0 pm	Enemy put a barrage on BERTHA Post + attempted to rush it but was repulsed	
		11 pm	After an intense bombardment the enemy succeeded in driving our garrison out of BERTHA Post which he then occupied	
		7.45 pm	Enemy attacked ENFIELD Post but was driven off with the help of a supporting platoon, a barrage fire from Stokes mortars + artillery	
	Jan 23	4.30 am	BERTHA Post reoccupied by us	
			Situation normal. Considerable hostile artillery activity. Hostile artillery active all day	
	Jan 24	7.0 pm	Enemy commenced an intense bombardment of Bertha Post. An infantry attack	
		7.50 pm	Enemy attempted to reach BARNET Post had repulsed	
		8.59 pm	Enemy again attacked BARNET Post in force. They were driven off with the help of supporting troops who immediately reinforced the post.	
			IRMA Post also attacked but enemy repulsed.	
			Enemy artillery fire very heavy causing us considerable casualties.	

WAR DIARY
or
INTELLIGENCE SUMMARY.
(Erase heading not required.)

Army Form C. 2118.

Place	Date	Hour	Summary of Events and Information	Remarks and references to Appendices
La Gorgue	Jan 25		Situation again normal. Artillery action on both sides. Weather still very cold	
	Jan 26		Quiet day. 167 Inf Bde relieved 168 Inf Bde in accordance with Divisional Operation Order No 65 - Appendix I	Appendix I
	Jan 27		Ismail Post again heavily bombarded by the enemy at 4 pm. Garrison withdraws. The enemy did not establish just N of Irish Salient.) Ground still frozen about 5 am. New post established.	
	28		Quiet day. Patrol encounter at night	
	29		During the preceding night the permanent garrisons of the posts, with drawn and all stores etc brought back. Quiet day. Some hostile shelling of evacuated posts.	
	30		Some artillery and TM activity on both side. One patrol entered the German lines at several new points & found them unoccupied. Major General Hull reassumed command of the Division	
	31		Artillery activity. XI Corps Operation Order No 95 received to take over the Section held by the 111th Bde & 31st Divn. Divisional Operation order No 66 issued accordingly	Appendix I

Appendix I

SECRET.   Copy No. 21

56th DIVISIONAL ORDER No. 66.
                                                     31st January 1917.

WITHDRAWAL OF 37th DIVISION.	1.	The 37th Division is to be relieved by 5th and 56th Division.
RELIEF.	2.	(a) 168th Infantry Brigade will relieve the 111th Infantry Brigade in the NEUVE CHAPELLE Section on 1st & 2nd February, the relief to be complete by daylight on 3rd February. All details of relief will be arranged direct between Brigadiers concerned. Brigade H.Q. will be at LES 8 MAISONS. (b). The relief of the Brigade M.G.Coy. will be carried out on 1st February after midday. (c). The 168th L.T.M.Battery will relieve on 1st February after midday.
BOUNDARY.	3.	The boundary between 5th and 56th Divisions will be BOND ST. S. - S.9.a.9.6. - S.9.d.4.4.- M.32.d.6.3. - M.31.a.0.0. all inclusive to 56th Division. 5th Division will have the use of EDWARD ROAD in addition to 56th Division.
ARTILLERY.	4.	(a). The new 56th Divisional front will be covered by the 56th Div. Arty. together with the 282nd F.A.Bde. (b). The 18 pr. batteries and 4.5" How. Sections of the 282nd F.A.Bde. at present attached to 37th Divn. will come under the orders of 56th Division on completion of the relief. (c). The relief will take place on the nights 1st/2nd and 2nd/3rd February, 4 guns of each battery being relieved on the first night and two on the second night. Such enfilade Sections as are to be relieved will be relieved on the first night, but an Officer, one Sergeant and four other ranks of the relieved section are to remain with the incoming Section until 24 hours after the relief. (d). Guns will not be exchanged, but aiming posts will be left in position, and the relieving battery or Section will hand over an equivalent to the outgoing battery or section. number (e). Group H.Q. will be at R.29 central.
R.E. & PIONEERS.	5.	The 513th (2/2nd London) Fld. Coy. R.E. and two platoons 1/5th Cheshire Regiment (Pioneers) will be attached to 168th Infantry Brigade. These will relieve on 2nd February under arrangements to be made by the C.R.E.

Appendix I

2.

STORES.	6.	All trench stores, maps, defence schemes, aeroplane photographs, etc. will be taken over on relief.
POSTS.	7.	A map showing the Posts in each Brigade Area on the new Divisional front is attached.

All Posts in rear of and including the VILLAGE LINE will be furnished with caretakers of not less than 3 O.R. each.

G.O.C's Infantry Brigades will mutually arrange to take over such posts in their respective areas as are now furnished by other Brigades.

169th Infantry Brigade will find the caretaking party for GRAND PACAUT and PONT RIQUEUL.

COMMAND. 8. G.O.C., 168th Infantry Brigade will assume Command of the NEUVE CHAPELLE Section on completion of the relief.

REPORTS. 9. Progress of relief will be reported to Div. H.Q.

10. ACKNOWLEDGE

B Pakenham
Lieut-Colonel,
General Staff.

Head Qrs. 56th Divn.

Issued at 2.30 pm

Copy No.
1. 167th Infantry Bde.
2. 168th " "
3. 169th " "
4. 5th Division
5. 37th Division
6 & 7. XI Corps
8. C.R.A.
9. C.R.E.
10. 1/5th Cheshire Regt.
11. A.D.M.S.
12. "Q"
13. A.P.M.
14. 193rd Div.M.G.Coy.
15. Sect. 15th Bty.M.M. G.C.
16. 56th Div. Signals.
17. 56th Div. Train.
18. Div. Machine Gun Offr.
19. 257th Tunnelling Coy.
20. G.O.C.
21. War Diary
22. File.

POSTS

SECRET

- Cable Line
- Front Line
- Reserve Lines
- Village Line

Appendix I

SECRET.   Copy No. 19

56th DIVISIONAL ORDER No. 63.

29th December, 1916.

1. The 168th Infantry Brigade will relieve the 169th Infantry Brigade in the MOATED GRANGE Section on the 2nd, and 3rd January, 1917, the relief to be completed by 6.0 p.m. on 3rd January.

2. The relief of the 169th Machine Gun Company will be carried out on 1st January by 168th Machine Gun Company and one section (4 guns) 193rd Divisional Machine Gun Company. The section 193rd Machine Gun Company will be placed under the orders of the General Officer Commanding MOATED GRANGE Section.

3. The 193rd Divisional Machine Gun Company will also place a section (4 guns) under the orders of the General Officer Commanding FAUQUISSART Section on 1st January.

4. The relief of Light Trench Mortar Batteries will be carried out on 1st January.

5. Arrangements will be made between the Brigades concerned so that the usual infantry working parties are provided daily during the relief.

6. All details of relief etc., will be arranged between the Brigades concerned.

7. Progress of relief will be reported daily to Divisional Headquarters.

8. ACKNOWLEDGE.

Pakenham

Lieut. Colonel,
General Staff.

Hdqrs. 56th Divn.

Issued at 6.30 a.m.

Copy No.
1. XIth Corps.
2. 5th Divn.
3. New Zealand Div.
4. 37th Divn.
5. 167th Inf. Bde.
6. 168th   "   "
7. 169th   "   "
8. C. R. E.
9. "Q".
10. Div. Signals.
11. Div. Schools.
12. Divnl. Train.
13. 56th Div. Arty
14. A.D.M.S.
15. A.P.M.
16. G.O.C. 56th Divn.
17. 257th Tunnelling Co. R.E.
18. 15th M.M.G. Coy.
19. War Diary.
20. 5th Ches. Regt.
21. Div. Training Bttn.
22 & 23. File.
23. 193rd (Div.) M.G. Coy.

Appendix I

SECRET. Copy No. 18

56th DIVISIONAL ORDER No. 64.

10th January 1917.

1. The 169th Infantry Brigade will relieve the 167th Infantry Brigade in the FAUQUISSART SECTION on 13th & 14th January, 1917, the relief to be completed by midnight 14th/15th.

2. The relief of 167th M.G. Coy. and one Section 193rd M.G. Coy. will be carried out on 12th January by 169th M.G. Coy. and one Section 193rd M.G. Coy.

3. The relief of L.T.M. Batteries will be carried out on 12th January.

4. Arrangements will be made between the Brigades concerned so that the cessation of work by infantry working parties does not exceed 24 hours.

5. All details of relief, etc. will be arranged between Brigades concerned.

6. Progress of relief will be reported daily to Divisional Headquarters.

7. ACKNOWLEDGE.

B. Pakenham
Lieut-Colonel,
General Staff.

Head Qrs. 56th Divn.

Issued at 10. a.m. 10/1/17

Copy No.

1.	XI Corps.	11.	Divnl. Train
2.	New Zealand Div.	12.	56th Div. Arty.
3.	37th Divn.	13.	A.D.M.S.
4.	167th Inf. Bde.	14.	A.P.M.
5.	168th Inf. Bde.	15.	G.O.C.56th Divn.
6.	169th Inf. Bde.	16.	257th Tunnelling Co.R.E.
7.	C.R.E.	17.	15th M.M.G.Coy.
8.	"Q"	18.	War Diary.
9.	Div. Signals.	19.	5th Ches. Regt.
10.	Div. Schools.	20.	Div.Training Bn.
		21	193rd (Div) M.G.Coy.
		22)	
		23)	File

Appendix 1

SECRET.   Copy No 18

AMENDMENT to 56th DIV. ORDER No. 64.

11th January, 1918.

The following amendments are made:-

Para. 1.   In line 2 for "13th and 14th January" substitute "14th January".

In line 3 for "midnight 14/15th" substitute "midnight 14th".

Para. 2.   In line 2 for "12th January" substitute "13th January".

Para. 3.   Substitute. The relief of the Light T.M. Batteries will be arranged between Brigades concerned.

ACKNOWLEDGE.

B Pakenham

Lieut. Colonel,
General Staff.

Hdqrs. 56th Divn.
        Issued at 2.30 p.m.

Copy No.

1. XI Corps
2. New Zealand Div.
3. 37th Divn.
4. 167th Inf. Bde.
5. 168th "   "
6. 169th "   "
7. C. R. E.
8. "Q".
9. Div. Signals.
10. Div. Schools.
11. Div. Train.
12. 56th Div. Arty.
13. A.D.M.S.
14. A.P.M.
15. G.O.C., 56th Divn.
16. 257th Tunnelling Co. RE.
17. 15th M.M.G. Coy.
18. War Diary.
19. 5th Ches. Regt.
20. Div. Training Bn.
21. 193rd (Div) M.G. Coy.
22 & 23. File.

Appendix I

SECRET.   Copy No. 18

56th DIVISIONAL ORDER No. 65.

                                                 22nd January, 1917.

1.   The 167th Infantry Brigade will relieve the 168th Infantry Brigade in the MAZINGARBE GRANGE Section on 26th January, the relief to be complete by midnight 26/27th.

2.   The relief of the 168th Machine Gun Company and one Section 193rd Machine Gun Company will be carried out on 25th January by 167th Machine Gun Company and one Section 193rd Machine Gun Company.

3.   The relief of light trench mortar batteries will be carried out on 25th January.

4.   All details of relief etc. will be arranged between Brigades concerned.

5.   Progress of relief will be reported daily to Divisional Headquarters.

6.   ACKNOWLEDGE.

                                                 B. Pakenham
                                                 Lieut. Colonel,
Hdqrs. 56th Divn.   General Staff.

         Issued at 2.30 p.m.

Copy No.
 1. XIth Corps.   13. A.D.M.S.
 2. New Zealand Div.   14. A.P.M.
 3. 37th Division.   15. G.O.C., 58th Divn.
 4. 167th Infantry Bde.   16. 257th Tunnelling Coy. R.E.
 5. 168th Infantry Bde.   17. 15th M.M.G. Coy.
 6. 169th Infantry Bde.   18. War Diary.
 7. C. R. E.   19. 5th Ches. Regt.
 8. "Q".   20. Div. Training Bn.
 9. Div. Signals.   21. 193rd (Div) M.G. Coy.
10. Divnl. Train.   22. Divnl. M.G. Officer.
11. Divnl. School.   23.) File.
12. 56th Div. Arty.   24.)

Appendix II

LOCATION TABLE FOR INFANTRY BRIGADES.

JANUARY

	1	2	3	4	5	6	7	8	9	10	11	12	13	14
167th Infantry Brigade														
Bde. H.Q.	LAVENTIE. M4b.2.6.													
1st London Regt.	L	LAVENTIE N							L	L	L	L	L	
3rd " "	LAVENTIE.S	R	R	R	R	R	R	LAVENTIE.S.						
7th Middlesex Regt.	R	LAVENTIE.S.						LAVENTIE.N, 2Coy. RUE DU BACQUEROT. 2Coy.	R	R	R	R	R	
8th "	LAVENTIE.N	L	L	L	L	L	L							
168th Infantry Brigade														
Bde. H.Q.	MERVILLE	LAVENTIE. COCK&HY HOUSE.												
4th London Regt.	BOUTDEVILLE	RIEZ BAILLEUL							R	R	R	R	R	
12th " (Rangers)	ROBERMETZ	PONT DU HEM	L	L	L	L	L	Pont du Hem	R	R	R	R	R	
13th " (Kens.)	GD.PACAUT	RIEZ BAILLEUR	R	R	R	R	R	Riez Bailleul	L	L	L	L	L	
14th " (Lon.Sc.)	LA GORGUE	PONT DU HEM							L	L	L	L	L	
169th Infantry Brigade														
Bde. H.Q.	LAVENTIE	MERVILLE												
2nd London Regt. (R.F.)	L	LA GORGUE												
5th " " (LRB)	RIEZ BAILLEUL	GRAND PACAUT												
9th " " (QVR)	PONT DU HEM	ROBERMETZ												
16th " " (QWR)	R	R	BOUTDEVILLE											

NOTE:—

Battalions in the trenches   RED
Battalions in Support   BLACK
Brigade in Reserve   GREEN

LEFT SECTION   N.8.d.05.85 to M.24.d.15.65   Bn. Boundary N.13.c.7.9.
RIGHT SECTION M.24.d.15.65 " M.35.d.55.65   Bn. Boundary M.29.d.95.80.

Appendix II

LOCATION TABLE FOR INFANTRY BRIGADES

— JANUARY —

	14	15	16	17	18	19	20	21	22	23	24	25	26
167th Infantry Brigade													
Bde. H.Q.	Merville												Lavantie
1st London Regiment.	La Gorgue												Riez Bailleul
3rd "	Robermetz												R
7th Middlesex Regt.	Pont Levantie												Pont du Hem
8th "	Le Paceur												"
168th Infantry Brigade													
Bde. H.Q.	Lavantie	Cockshy House											Merville
4th London Regt.	R	Riez Bailleul			L	L	L	R	R	R	R	R	La Gorgue
12th " (Rangers.)	Pont du Hem	R			R	R	R	L	L	L	L	L	Robermetz
13th " (Kens.)	Riez Bailleul	L			R	R	R	L	L	L	L	R	Bout Deville
14th " (Lon.Sc.)	L	Pont du Hem			L	L	L	R	R	R	R	L	grand Pacaul
169th Infantry Brigade													
Bde. H.Q. (E.F.)	Lavantie	M4b 2.6.			L	L	L	R	R	R	R	R	Lavantie
2nd London Regt. (LRB)	L	L			R	R	R	L	L	L	L	L	Lavantie
5th " (QVR)	Lavantie + 2 coys Rue Bacqueret	L			L	L	L	R	R	R	R	L	Lavantie
9th " (QWR)	Lavantie	R			R	R	R	L	L	L	L	R	"
16th "	R	R			R	R	R	R	R	R	R	R	Lavantie (2 coys Rue du Bacquerot)

NOTE.— Battalions in the trenches   RED
          Battalions in Support   BLACK
          Brigade in Reserve   GREEN

LEFT SECTION N.8.d.05.85 to M.24.d.15.65   Bn. Boundary N.13.c.7.9.
       "   M.24.d.15.65 " M.35.d.55.65   Bn. Boundary M.29.d.95.80.
RIGHT

Appendix II

LOCATION TABLE FOR INFANTRY BRIGADES.

	JANUARY					FEBRUARY															
	27	28	29	30	31	1	2	3	4	5	6	7	8	9	10	11	12	13	14	15	16
167th Infantry Brigade.																					
Bde. H.Q.	Lavenlie Cockyshy House	L	L	L	L																
1st London Regt.	Rieg Bailleul	L	L	L	L																
3rd " "		R	R	R	R																
7th Middlesex Regt.	Pont du Hem	R	R	R	R																
8th " "																					
168th Infantry Brigade.																					
Bde. H.Q.	Merville																				
4th London Regt.	La Gorgue																				
12th " (Rangers).	Robermetz																				
13th " (Kens.)	Beul Deuile																				
14th " (Lond.Scot.)	Grand Flamet																				
169th Infantry Brigade.																					
Bde. H.Q.	Lavenlie	L	L	L	L	L	Lavenlie														
2nd London Regt. (R.F.)	Lavenlie + Rue Bacqueret	L	L	L	L	L	R	R	R	R	R										
5th " " (L.R.B.)	Lavenlie R	R	R	R	R	R	R	L	L	L	L										
9th " " (QWR.)		R	R	R	R	R	R	L	L	L	L										
16th " " (QWR.)	R	R	R	R	R	R	R	Lavenlie + Rue Bacqueret													

NOTE:- Battalions in the trenches   RED.
        Battalions in support   BLACK.
        Brigade in reserve.   GREEN.

Left Section N.8.d.05.85. to M.24.d.15.65. Bn. Boundary N.13.c.7.9.
Right Section M.24.d.15.65. " M.35.d.55.65. Bn. Boundary M.29.d.95.80.

Appendix III

**56th DIVISIONAL TACTICAL PROGRESS REPORT No. 66
from 8.0 a.m. 31st December to 8.0 a.m. 1st January 1917.**

On receipt of current copy of Divisional Tactical Progress Report
in the trenches, previous copy to be destroyed.

PART I OPERATIONS.

RIGHT SECTION.- Two bombardments in short bursts were carried out against enemy's C.Ts. and roads at dusk and at 10.55 p.m. last night, with a view to catching enemy W.Ps. moving up and disturbing any New Year celebrations. From 10.a.m. to 4.p.m. a slow observed bombardment by Heavy and Medium T.Ms. was carried out against enemy T.Ms. in M.30.a. and trenches M.30.a.9.3. and M.30.c.6.7.- results were good, much material damage being observed.

Our M.Gs. combined with the artillery bombardments and carried out the usual night firing.

One of our patrols was fired upon from enemy lines about M.36.c.0.5. Enemy wire was inspected for 200 yards opposite SHORD TRENCH and found to be much damaged by our fire. A large hostile working party was located and L.Gs. were brought to bear on it.

A telephone wire buried about a feet deep was found entering our parapet at M.30.a.40.88. The wires were traced into the ditch running from M.30.a.40.94. to M.30.a.90.56. and for about 70 yards along the ditch where the wire was lost.

LEFT SECTION.- At midnight our T.Ms bombarded enemy lines at N.14.c.3.4. without drawing any retaliation.

Our M.G.s were active throughout the night, firing on back areas.

German trenches were entered as follows :-
1. At junction of DORA C.T. and front line and line found in a very bad state.
2. Immediately S. of WICK SALIENT.
3. A standing patrol was established in the German front line in front of TRIVELET. They heard sounds of working near N.19.b.1.5. during the early part of the night.
   All patrols report Very lights were being fired from 300-500 yards in front of them.
4. Snipers have been established in the hostile front line at N.13.c.9.2. to wait for targets today.
5. At N.13.d.8.7. the line was found to be five feet deep in mud and water and water has risen considerably everywhere since the night before.
6. At N.14.c.25.85. enemy line is reported in fairly good condition except that the water is up to the fire step.
7. The wire at N.8.d.2.1. is now reported completely cut and the saps waterlogged.

The opportunity is being taken of sending out all fresh men who have not been on patrol before and much instruction is being given.

A sniper claims a victim who was seen to fall forward and has not moved since.

PART II INTELLIGENCE.

RIGHT SECTION.- Hostile Artillery was fairly active and retaliated with some effect for our T.M. Bombardment. Our front line, C.T.s and B. Line all received some attention. Retaliation for our 10.55pm bombardment was also prompt but no damage was done. Back areas were shelled during the day, the roads round LA FLINQUE and PONT DU HEM being fired over.

Hostile M.G.s were more active than usual traversing our parapets by night. A night emplacement is suspected at M.36.c.4.7. Hostile T.M.s were active in the Right Subsection - the Heavy mortars opening fire twice on M.29.2. Artillery retaliation was vigorous and effective.

2.

PART II INTELLIGENCE (continued)
LEFT SECTION. - Heavy Artillery fired some H.E. on front line without doing any damage. A hostile T.M. was observed to fire 6 rounds from enemy support line at N.14.c.10.55 and another battery was reported in action from N.14.a.70.09. A new M.G. Emplacement is suspected at N.14.b.20.88.

New wood can be seen at N.22.c.8.7. (FROMELLES DEFENCES) and N.27.a.75.60. (AUBERS DEFENCES). Fresh earth has been thrown up in hostile second line at N.13.d.85.50.

Much movement was seen during the day and many parties dispersed by our Artillery.

A party at Road Junction N.26.c.5.7. was dispersed with shrapnel.

A Working Party on the new trench in N.32.a. was dispersed with by Howitzer and Gun fire. The CLIQUETERIE FARM Road was in use during the day and three parties of 30 men and six of 12 men were seen to pass moving N.E. shortly after 11.0 a.m. Artillery was informed.

At 14 TREES CLUMP.
   N.21.a.88.70   small parties moving S.E. along the tramway.
   N.15.c.05.70
TRAMWAY CORNER.
   About AUBERS DEFENCES N.22.c., N.21.d. and N.27.a.   2 men laying lines at N.21.d.2.1.
   N.25.d.7.5.   Party of 12 men carrying brushwood.
   N.20.d.75.32   9 men carrying shovels.
   N.14.d.90.55   9 men.
   several other smaller parties.

ARTILLERY.
At 5. p.m. the flashes of 2 guns were seen and they were thought to be about N.25.c. central.
   N.34.a.50.65   No. 149 Battery reported at 11.30 a.m. firing on N.13.a.
   N.28.d.4.2.   No. 159 was again seen yesterday and is a 77 mm. battery firing N. and N.W.

6 trucks were seen standing on the AUBERS-FROMELLES Rly. E. of FERME DU HOYON and 5 trucks W. of the Farm.

SMOKE.
   N.27.a.55.50)
   N.21.d.05.00) AUBERS DEFENCES.

   N.20.d.7.6.   House.
   N.20.d.5.8.   House.   Direct hits obtained.
   N.20.b.30.55   Trench.
   N.15.a.1.5.   Chimney.

Head Qrs. 56th Divn.
1st January 1917.

Captain,
Intelligence, General Staff.

56th DIVISIONAL TACTICAL PROGRESS REPORT No. 47.
from 8.0 a.m 1st January to 8.0 a.m. 2nd January 1917.

On receipt of current copy of Divisional Tactical Progress Report
in the trenches, previous copy to be destroyed.

PART I OPERATIONS.

RIGHT SECTION.- At 1.p.m. the enemy commenced an organised bombardment which opened with a quarter of an hour's rapid distributed over the whole of our front. It is apparent from the list of targets engaged that the enemy had obtained a fair knowledge of our "tender spots" from observation extending over the last month Our artillery quickly retaliated on to enemy front and support line. When it was evident that the enemy was carrying out an organised "shoot", which local fire was quite powerless to check, a short programme for Group Artillery in conjunction with 6" hows. and 4.7" was arranged for 3.0 p.m. This succeeded in stopping his fire to a very large extent, but steady fire on back areas was continued till dusk, a large number of lachrymatory shells falling on the line of the RUE BACQUEROT. A retaliatory bombardment has been arranged to take place today.
Our M.Gs. showed their usual night activity.
One of our patrols examined the buildings at N.35.d.8.7. on their S. and W. fronts. They form a hollow square with pit in centre full of water. None of the enemy were encountered. Another patrol examined the enemy wire opposite N.29.3. They heard two or three men walking through water in the enemy trench, halting occasionally for a few moments. It appears, therefore, that this portion of the enemy line is merely patrolled. Other patrols could find no signs of the enemy

LEFT SECTION.- Our artillery replied affectively to the enemy's bombardment during the afternoon, whilst our M.Gs. sprayed the enemy's wire and trenches intermittently throughout the night especial attention being paid to the Cross Roads at N.20.a.8.7. Patrols were sent out last night to investigate the following points:-
(1) Junction of BERTHA TRENCH and front line
(2) Junction of IRMA and front line
(3) SUGAR LOAF
In all 12 patrols went out during the night but only 2 were able to penetrate the enemy's front line owing to the state of the ground although bridging was employed. At N.13.d.9.7. an Officers' patrol entered the German line by the Sap and Crater. Each were found unoccupied, the former in a bad state and the latter full of water but a few bombs were found about Saphead. Very few strands of wire were found at this point. Patrol moved South along parapet to point N.13.d.68.58. - trench was in good condition, wood revetted but water was above fire step which was about 3 ft. high. Wire was quite good here, and three groups of bombs were found. Patrols returned with spade bombs and box periscope. A further patrol under the same officer worked N. from Crater to N.14.c.15. 73. Trench good in most places but same level of water. At N.14.c.10.70. an open M.G. Emplacement was found with a pile of empty cartridge cases. This is the only point so far which has been found to have communication to the rear, duck boards being laid across the water. Sap nearby was unoccupied. Another patrol visited these parts about 2 hours later but nothing was seen or heard of the enemy. Six separate attempts were made to examine trenches at the head of IRMA not a sound was heard of the enemy. Two patrols attempted to enter the S. side of the SUGAR LOAF but failed. They worked with the battalion on our left.
The three snipers who had remained in the German front line at N.13.c.9.2. all day report that the German front line trench is on the far side of the River LAIES running parallel to it from 50 to 100 yards distant. They state that the ground between the old German front line and the River LAIES is like a lake dotted with islands. They could see no points capable of being held by the enemy. No passages across the water could be perceived and no bridges across the LAIES to the RUE D'ENFER.

P.T.O.
/No.

No movement or targets were seen, but there appeared to be much new work on the trench across the river LAIES.

PART II INTELLIGENCE.
RIGHT SECTION.- During the bombardment mentioned above it is estimated that the enemy fired over 1,300 shells of all calibres. His trench mortars co-operated and a number of Heavy and Medium Shells fell along the front line - damage was not great.
Considerable movement during the day was seen on the screened road AUBERS - CAS POMMEREAU.. Work was being carried on at N.25.c. 6.2. and at the Railway at M.30.d.45.60. Two men walked from CAS POMMEREAU to WIRELESS HOUSE T.2.b.2.7. at 12 noon.

LEFT SECTION.- In the afternoon hostile shelling became very heavy reaching its maximum about 2.45 p.m. first on front line then on RUE TILLELOY and Reserve Line lifting to RUE BACQUEROT. The shells fired were mainly 4.2" or 5.9" including a quantity of gas and tear shells. A great number of flashes were observed coming from Wood at N.27.c.8.5. and from behind Wood at N.17.d.5.5. The hostile battery at N.28.d.4.2. was again in action. The hostile T.Ms. were active during the bombardment. At 1.0 p.m. the trench mortar at N.14.c.1.5½. fired 15 rounds, and another trench mortar about 20 yards to its right was also firing. A heavy T.M. was located at N.14.d.95.65.
Fresh earth and timber are reported on CLARA C.T. at N.19.d.15.95. About 8.0 a.m. a party of Germans was seen to dump coils of wire about N.19.b.9.2. They went off in an Easterly direction entering BERTHA C.T. at N.20.b.3.0. At this point a sentry could be seen looking over the top. New work has been done on the emplacement about N.14.b.2.8. New wire and stakes have been erected at N.26.a.3.2. and N.20.d. 7.72. About 1.45 a.m. a party of 10 Germans came from behind the hedge at N.14.d.1.4. and disappeared at N.20.a.87.63. A glass was seen moving from side to side in slit in roof of house at N.26.d.60.65. Usual movement was seen at N.20.b.30.65. and AUBERS DEFENCES.
Smoke was seen at N.20.b.35.5. Headquarters Dugout.
N.21.d.40.15. AUBERS DEFENCES.
N.27.a.5.3. House.

[signature]

Lieutenant,
Intelligence, General Staff.

Head Qrs. 56th Divn.
2nd January, 1917.

56th DIVISIONAL TACTICAL PROGRESS REPORT No. 38.
from 8.0 a.m. 2nd January to 8.0 a.m. 3rd January 1917.

On receipt of current copy of Divisional Tactical Progress Report in the trenches, previous copy to be destroyed.

Part 1 OPERATIONS.

RIGHT SECTION.- An organised bombardment took place from 10 a.m. to 3. p.m. on enemy front line, where it was not being treated by T.Ms. with special attention to suspected mine shafts; support and reserve lines- C.Ts., tramways and cross roads.

Group artillery fired 1,000 rounds and 3" Hows. 100 rounds, while Heavy and Light T.Ms. co-operated on occupied positions of their front line system, with 10 and 400 rounds respectively. Much damage was done, woodwork being thrown up and bombstore at M.30.d.15.60 was hit. Enemy's retaliation at this period was negligible.

At 3.40 p.m. hostile artillery fired a burst of rapid fire and we retaliated vigorously. The front was covered by patrols and advanced listening posts, but no signs of the enemy were seen.

LEFT SECTION.- Between 1.0 p.m. and 3.0 p.m. our artillery fired a series of sharp bursts on enemy C.Ts. and strong points as per programme. We also retaliated energetically for enemy's shelling at 4.40 p.m. and 6.0 p.m. and he was quickly silenced on each occasion.

Usual night firing was carried out by M.Gs.
Enemy's front line was searched by our patrols last night and no signs of occupation found.

PART II INTELLIGENCE.

RIGHT SECTION.- Hostile retaliation to our midday shoot was weak, but at 3.30 p.m. a short intense bombardment of the Left Sub-section took place. Damage was slight. Of 25 shells that fell near the CHORD only 6 exploded.

Hostile T.Ms. were not as active as usual.

A M.G. suspected at M.24.d.70.17 opened on an aeroplane working with the heavies.

A hostile W.P. just S. of the MAUQUISSART Crater was dispersed by L.G. fire. There was less movement than usual yesterday, but a party at T.2.c. was dispersed by field guns and good shooting was done by L.T.Ms. on N.35.d.9'.3. where movement had been seen.

LEFT SECTION.- From 6 to 6.10 p.m. an intense bombardment with guns of all calibres plus T.Ms. was carried out against our lines. Targets were :- Front line from M.24.4 to N.13.1 (both inclusive) with
    WANGERIE AV.)   field guns.
    ELGIN ST.)
    ELGIN POST)   H.T.Ms., 4.2" and 5.9" H.E.
    Rt.& Centre Coy.H.Q.)

At the same time the left battalion front and reserve lines were bombarded fairly heavily. A party of 50 was seen in AUBERS N.27.a.6.3. moving towards FROMELLES at 8.30 a.m. There was much movement throughout the day round houses at N.14.d.90.55 and N.20.a.87.63. Two men were seen at 1.10 p.m. carrying a large round polished tin about 4 ft. long by 2ft diameter across a field N.32.d. An O.P. is suspected in the fifth tree of the clump to the right of house at N.20.a.87.63. Fresh work has been done at N.22.c.36.10, N.22.b.50.35. and N.22.b.45.20 and revetting can be seen at these spots. New sandbags can be seen on the small blind trench at N.20.b.03.30. and men were seen looking over the top here. There was considerable movement in N.21.d. during the day. The usual sentry movements were seen in trench N.20.b.30.55. The following parties were dispersed by our artillery :-

On track N.15.c.65.32 - N.15.c.4.2. A party of 12 and several smaller parties at intervals.

5 men working on AUBERS - FROMELLES Road at N.27.b.90.85.
Two parties of 4 men each drawing timber from dump at N.14.b.85.00.
At 4.25 p.m. the H.T.M. was again seen firing from N.14.d.95.65 on to our front line N.14.1. and N.8.1.
Our artillery quickly silenced it.

58th DIVISIONAL TACTICAL PROGRESS REPORT 69
from 8.0 a.m. 3rd January to 8.0 a.m. 4th January 1917.

On receipt of current copy of Divisional Tactical Progress Report
in the trenches, previous copy to be destroyed.

PART I OPERATIONS.

LEFT SECTION.- Our artillery carried out a small organised shoot on enemy billets at N.20.b.33.40. The result seemed effective. Working parties at N.20.c.10.10 and N.21.d.55.20 were dispersed. No targets are available for our L.T.Ms. Our M.Gs. were very active during the day and night with indirect fire. Targets being chiefly in LE PIETRE. Our patrols entered the only points in the German front line from just S. of SUGAR LOAF to DORA C.T. which had not previously been examined, viz about N.14.a.5½.0 - N.19.a.5.8½ and N.19.c.2.9. The German front and support lines N.W. of the river LAIES are flooded out and abandoned except at the SUGAR LOAF and just at the junctions of BERTHA C.T. and IRMA C.T. with the support line, where there are posts. Further confirmation is required of the exact positions of these occupied positions. It is also thought that there is a post in CLARA C.T. at N.19.a.9.5. The patrol which entered the German line at N.19.c.2.9. report the trench to have about 1 ft. of water in it. They found a concrete dugout with water in, and they saw a light at about N.19.c.2.6. The enemy wire there is smashed up. At 12.15 p.m. our snipers claim to have hit a German at N.8.d.30.10.

RIGHT SECTION.- Our artillery was quiet and our T.Ms. were chiefly engaged in ranging and testing new base plates. A small practice shoot was held on the left. Our patrols reported (1) that our wire in front of our left sub-section is thick and affords a good obstacle. (2) That the enemy's wire and parapet opposite M.24.2 is in bad repair, a deep ditch runs along parallel to the German trenches and makes it impossible to get very close. (3) That there is a German listening post in the Crater at M.30.c.4.0.

PART II INTELLIGENCE

LEFT SECTION.- Hostile Artillery and T.Ms. were inactive, there being no retaliation to our shoot. A few light shells fell in rear of N.8.1 without doing any damage. Much work is going on in the German second line defences between AUBERS and FROMELLES, and it is thought that is the front line trenches have been abandoned. supporting troops now occupy this line, smoke is continually being observed in various places.

At 9.30 a.m. a party of 20 men were observed working at N.21.d.45.15. Our artillery fired on them. Much new work is visible here, and work was being continued during the afternoon. At 10.30 a.m. transport coming from AUBERS halted at N.27.a.80.38 and unloaded 10 feet planks into the trench by the road. Smoke was seen at N.21.c.95.15. and N.23.a.87.72. A large party of about 3 officers and 80 men were erecting wire entanglements and digging between N.20.c.10.10 and N.20.c.99.99 about 7.50 a.m. The officers were wearing greatcoats with capes and peaked caps and the men in clear fatigue. Our artillery were warned. Work was seen at N.25.d.7.5. New work was done on IRMA C.T. at N.14.b.30.15 and BERTHA C.T. at N.20.a.9.8. Thirty men in all were seen about N.20.a.87.63. and disappearing at N.20.b.05.90. Smoke was seen at :-

    N.20.a.87.63   house
    N.23.a.87.72   trench
    N.14.d.33.48   trench

RIGHT SECTION.- Hostile artillery and T.Ms. were quiet. A party wearing a white band on their left arm were seen building a screen at N.25.c.9.6. - they were dispersed by our artillery. Usual movement was observed on the LA CLIQUETERIE Fm.Road in T.3.a. Considerable movement was observed in the new trench in N.26.c. to N.32.a. Fired on by our artillery.

Head Qrs. 58th Divn.
4th January, 1917.

T.J.C.Heald Lieutenant,
Intelligence, General Staff.

56th DIVISIONAL TACTICAL PROGRESS REPORT, No. 70
from 8.0 a.m. 4th January to 8.0 a.m. 5th January, 1917.

On receipt of current copy of Divisional Tactical Progress Report
in the trenches, previous copy to be destroyed.

PART I OPERATIONS.

RIGHT SECTION.- At 10.23 a.m. and 12.20 p.m. our artillery fired on the enemy front and support lines and C.Ts. in retaliation to enemy shelling. Our T.Ms. fired on M.36.a. good results being obtained.

Our patrols reported (1) That the enemy's parapet is badly damaged between M.30.b.2.8. and M.24.d.6.3. (2) Ground round the Craters at M.30.a.35.40 explored and is flooded. (3) No sign of the enemy found or heard.

LEFT SECTION.- Our artillery carried out an organised shoot on CLARA C.T. from N.19.a.94.29 to N.19.d.90.00. with good results. Our L.T.Ms. fired on point N.13.d.85.50. where new work has been observed and a hostile T.M. firing from close by. Our M.Gs. were active with indirect fire on the enemy's communications.

One of our patrols entered the German trenches N.13.c.9.8. where it is much damaged and flooded. They worked left to N.13.c.95.30 and from there pushed forward to the support line which is also full of water. Beyond was a sheet of water. Before reaching the support line the patrol had crossed a tramway and a dump where there was a large quantity of wire lying about. In the front line they found what appeared to be a spring gun which they tried to remove but failed. In addition they found and brought back a large bell, probably a gas alarm, a number of rifle and hand grenades, a pair of wire cutters, and a periscope. No signs of the enemy were seen or heard.

Another patrol attempted to enter at N.14.a.5½.1½. but were stopped by a deep ditch full of water and wire about 10 yards from the parapet. The wire here is thick in parts and the parapet much damaged. A dog was heard to bark from the post at the head of IRMA C.T. in N.14.b.4.0. A M.G. was firing from about N.14.c.3.3. A strong iron frame about 2 feet square was brought back from about 10 yards in front of the enemy's wire. The frame was wired with new wire.

Other patrols report no signs of the enemy.

A large box periscope was observed in enemy second line at N.14.a.9.2¼. It was smashed by our snipers.

PART II INTELLIGENCE.

RIGHT SECTION.- During the morning the enemy bombarded the support and reserve lines of the Right Battalion but no damage was done. The hostile T.Ms. carried out some very accurate shooting yesterday, and destroyed one of our T.M Emplacements, and badly damaged a mine. It is essential that bearings on them be taken from various parts of the line by sentries and observers so that these emplacements can be located accurately.

At 12.30 p.m. two men were seen at N.32.c.25.85. mending a telephone cable. Two steel plates are built in enemy parapet at M.30.c.50.55. A small party of the enemy were seen at M.36.c.25.80. - one man was hit by our snipers. A large cloud of white smoke was seen at this point later. Four men running towards the trench at N.32.b.1.9. were fired on by our artillery. Smoke was seen at N.35.a.3.3. and M.30.b.10.50.

LEFT SECTION.- Hostile artillery scattered a few shells over our support and rear lines without doing much damage. Hostile T.Ms. were silent.

The work on the trench behind the AUBERS-BAS POMMEREAU Road from N.26.c. to N.32.a. is being continued. Our artillery fired on a working party here and scattered them. One man was clearly seen to be limping.

Considerable movement was observed yesterday in N.21.a. Just before dusk 50 men in all were seen on track at N.21.a.70.75.

/Our

Left Section (contd).

Our artillery fired on them but light was too bad for observation.
Six other men were seen to leave trench at N.21.a.9.7. and disappear in a N.E. direction.

At N.14.b.80.55. four lengths of tram rails have been dumped.

Twenty men in clean fatigue walked along RUE DELEVAL from N.14.d.8.5. to N.14.d.30.35.

Usual movement observed on LA CLIQUETERIE Mt. Road.

At 10.30 a.m. 3 men, one carrying a black board apparently heavy and about 3 ft square, were seen by Willows at N.20.c.85. 75. They placed the board in the willows as a screen and then disappeared behind the willows.

Smoke was seen at:-
N.21.d.40.15. dugout.
N.21.b.85.05
N.22.c.95.48
N.14.d.25.60
N.15.c.00.65 SUSA's House
N.13.b.3.5. Trench.

Head Qrs. 56th Divn.
5th January, 1917.

F.P.Kald
Lieutenant,
Intelligence, General
Staff.

56th DIVISIONAL TACTICAL PROGRESS REPORT No. 71
from 8.0 a.m. 5th January to 8.0 a.m. 6th January 1917.

P. On receipt of current copy of Divisional Tactical Progress Report
in the trenches, previous copy to be destroyed.

PART I OPERATIONS.

RIGHT SECTION.- Our Artillery fired on working parties in
retaliation to hostile Trench Mortar fire. Good shooting was
done by L.T.M.s against enemy front and support lines, timber
and rails being thrown into the air. Hostile retaliation was
slight. There was some activity shown by enemy's snipers
opposite the right Battalion. Patrols forward the following
information :-
  (1) Sounds of work and talking in the enemy line opposite
      CHORD TRENCH.
  (2) Craters round A.30.a.5.5. are full of water.
  (3) Crater M.24.d.25.15. unoccupied.
NO MANS LAND flooded practically everywhere making progress
difficult. No hostile patrols met.

LEFT SECTION.- Our Artillery carried out registrations during
the day and a small shoot on the houses at N.25.b.80.93. Last
night two Stokes guns were placed in position in the enemy old
front line at N.19.a.30.65. and N.19.a.50.87. ?-a- Each gun
fired 20 rounds on the enemy strong point at the LOZENGE
N.19.a.9.5. as far as could be ascertained with good effect. There
was no retaliation. Our M.G.s were very active last night firing on
enemy communications and suspected supporting points.

A patrol .... left our lines for the purpose of exploring
the SUGAR LOAF - first objective N.8.d.30.02. could not be
reached owing to water but from this point to N.8.d.9.1. the
enemy trench is practically destroyed. At this point the
trench is well revetted. The trench - .. railway at N.8.d.33.10.
is still above water and unbroken at this point. There is a
truck on the line but it could not be reached owing to water.
There is every sign of the trench having been abandoned for some
time.

No position could be found from which L.T.M.s could be used as
there is 18" of soft mud in the .. driest places. Other patrols
were along the German line and confirm all previous reports.

PART II INTELLIGENCE.

RIGHT SECTOR.- Hostile Artillery was fairly active between 4.30. and
5.30.p.m. - shrapnel was fired over SIGN POST LANE. At 4.30.p.m,
"MINNIE" No.4 approximately M.30.d.4.2. opened fire. It was
silenced by our Artillery before any damage was done. A party
of 20 men were observed at M.30.b.25.80. and were dispersed by
L.G. Fire. Earth was being thrown over the parapet at M.30.c.5.6.
at noon and the artillery were put on to this target. A party
of 10 men carrying shovels seen at 10.30.a.m. N.25.c.8.4. Small
parties were seen at M.36.c.2.5. and fire opened on them. New
wire has been put out at M.24.d.48.15. and M.24.d.40.00.

LEFT SECTION. - Papers taken from the body of a dead German in
NO MANS LAND opposite the Right Subsection are forwarded. The
body is in a very advanced state of decomposition and the
identification 3rd Battn. 17th Reserve Infantry Regt. is now out
of date. Hostile artillery was quiet during the period, a few field
gun shells were fired at ROAD BEND POST. In the early
evening enemy M.G.s were unusually active. Enemy M.G.s opened fire
on one of our aeroplanes from their second line about D.14.c.85.85.
Work was being done yesterday morning in the enemy second line at
M.14.c.75.95. At 8.20.a.m. a German officer was seen to enter
ruined house - N.14.d.45.20. and to leave about five minutes later
accompanied by another officer. A red light was sent up from well
behind DEVIL'S JUMP at 5 p.m. and another at 9.p.m. Enemy balloon
ascended at 1.30.p.m. behind AUBERS but only remained up a quarter of
an hour.

Work on the trenches and wiring still continues in the AUBERS
DEFENCES. Fresh woodwork can be seen at N.21.d.22.10. and N.21.d.
54.18. Usual movement was seen during the day on the LA
CLIQUETERIE FM. Road, and also in the trench N.20.b.30.65. Usual

2.

LEFT SECTION (continued)
Usual movement was also seen on track N.21.d.9.7. - our artillery dispersed parties here.

Our artillery fired on a party of 6 men working on the AUBERS-FROMELLES Road.

During our T.M. bombardment yesterday morning 3 men were seen watching it from N.15.c.0.3. Six men were also seen by a small timber dump at N.15.c.45.20.

Smoke :-

        N.20.b.30.55.   Dugout.
        N.20.d.7.6.   House
        N.26.c.80.44   "
        N.15.a.70.26   "
        N.27.b.94.85   suspected sentry shelter on road
        M.30.d.9.8.   MIN DU PIETRE
        N.28.a.85.72   A dense cloud of smoke seen here at 12.30 p.m.

Head Qrs. 56th Divn.
6th January, 1917.

                                              Captain,
                                Intelligence, General Staff.

56th DIVISIONAL TACTICAL PROGRESS REPORT No. 72
from 8.0 a.m. 6th January to 8.0 a.m. January 7th 1917.

On receipt of current copy of Divisional Tactical Progress Report
in the trenches, previous copy to be destroyed.

PART I OPERATIONS.

LEFT SECTION.- Our artillery carried out a shoot on dykes with a view to further flooding enemy trenches about N.19.c.37.15. Our L.T.Ms. fired 50 rounds on N.8.d.30.15. from which point a M.G. was reported to be firing at 3. 0 p.m.

Our M.Gs. fired on to N.21.a.65.55 during the night.

A patrol examined the enemy trench and wire from M.24.d.9.6. to N.19.c.10.78 and has nothing new to report as regards the condition of the trench or wire. No signs of the enemy were seen or heard.

A patrol of 1 officer, 1 Sergeant, 1 Corporal and 3 men went out from the Central Company with the object of obtaining information as to whether the enemy had any posts West of river DES LAIES, and also information about the LOZENGE N.19.a.9.5.

The patrol crossed the German lines at N.19.a.25.50, and went from there to the tram-way. The tram-way was followed to N.19.a.45.35. where the patrol turned left striking the RIVER DES LAIES at N.19.a.75.40. The river is unfordable as the water is very deep, and there is barbed wire in it. Some of the patrol report sounds of coughing some distance away. They returned to the point N.19.a.45.30 crossing a narrow trench full of water on the way. They went along the railway to road at N.19.a.55.10. but at this point found it crosses the support line. The support line appears to be more of a trench than a breastwork and is full of water. The enemy front line is badly smashed up and the wire is very poor. The railway is broken in places and under mud and water. Where the tram-way crosses the ditch at N.19.a.5.3. it runs completely under a sheet of water 15 to 20 yards wide, and a truck is lying in the middle. This ditch is about waist deep. What was thought to be a snipers concrete dugout was found at N.19.a.35.40. It was impossible to enter it. At N.19.a.4.4. there was a good concrete dugout in which a machine gun could be placed to sweep the road and our front line. This dugout is lined with wood. A picture was taken out of this dugout. A bell and overcoat (Marked 17) were taken from a shelter dugout in the front line at N.19.a.40.35. A box of bombs were brought back. A box containing a curious instrument was found and brought back, also some iron rails from the railways.

At 10.30 p.m. a patrol entered the enemy front line at N.13.c.9 30. They secured and brought back the "spring gun" previously reported. When the mud had been removed from this it was found to be a rifle grenade standard. The patrol returned to the same point and penetrated as far as the support line which was found to be in the same flooded state. The enemy front line at WICK SALIENT was reconnoitred and a number of concrete dugouts were found intact, one of which had withstood a direct hit from one of our shells. Just N. of N.13.c.94.30. a fire bay was found which had apparently been a bombing bay or post, a wire being stretched the whole length of the bay and bombs hooked on to this wire.

A patrol consisting of 1 Officer and 16 Other ranks left our lines at 3.45 a.m. and proceeded across "NO MAN'S LAND" to the head of IRMA C.T. On arriving at about 10 yards from the above point footsteps were heard and two or three men were seen at the head of IRMA C.T. It was not found possible to get across at this point owing to the wide ditch which has barbed wire thrown in it. The patrol then moved 100 yards South with the idea of getting round to the back of these men but could not find a point where it was possible to get over the trench. The patrol returned at 6.0 a.m.

Another patrol left our lines at 8.30 p.m. to investigate the structure opposite RED LAMP, this proved to be a building of bricks about 12 ft. long, with a top layer of concrete and roofed with corrugated iron. It has no opening of any kind facing our lines and is thought to have been used for stores. The tren

2.

is very full of water at this point.

A further patrol went out at 7.0 p.m. and arrived at the enemy's lines at N.8.d.30.02. Here they turned S.W. and followed the line for about 90 yards. They report the wire here in a bad state of repair. No signs of the enemy were seen or heard, the ground was very heavy.

RIGHT SECTION.- Our artillery and H.T.Ms. carried out an offensive shoot on MOULIN DU PIETRE and EVA and FRIEDA C.Ts. Results were very satisfactory. Our T.Ms. fired on enemy wire around M.36.a.30.00. front line at M.30.b.35.95 and M.30.b.4.8. much damage was caused, a dugout is believed to have been destroyed, much timber and corrugated iron being thrown up. No retaliation.

Our patrols were out in front of this Section but did not come into contact with the enemy. They found the going difficult owing to water. The enemy wire round the Craters at M.30.a.central is exceptionally strong and is about 10 ft. in depth. The Craters are flooded. Our snipers had several targets and claimed 2 victims. At 4.0 p.m. 2 Germans mounted their parapet at M.36.c. 05.30. they were fired at and both fell. Two men passed a gap in the parapet at M.36.c.15.79. carrying a food container; they were fired at but result not ascertained.

PART II INTELLIGENCE.
LEFT SECTION.- Hostile artillery and T.Ms. were on the whole quiet.
A hostile machine gun was reported to be firing from N.14.c.35.05 during the night
A hostile party at N.25.b.80.93. was dispersed by our artillery.
Movement was observed at following points :-
    N.20.b.30.35   behind Willows.
    N.21.d.   AUBERS DEFENCES.
    N.21.a.9.7.   near IRMA C.T.
    T.3.a.   La CLIQUETERIE Fm. Road.
    N.20.b.30.55   Usual sentry over dugout in MOSSY C.T.

A smll A small black board can be seen in a tall tree at N.20.a. 85.40.
    Smoke was seen at :-
    N.20.d.50.85   House
    N.20.d.7.6.   "
    N.20.b.30.55   H.Q. dugout.

RIGHT SECTION. - Hostile artillery and T.Ms. showed some activity during the evening. At 9. 0 p.m. 4 H.T.Ms. fell behind right sub-section together with aerial torpedoes and light grenades. A bearing taken from one of our P.O.Ps. on the flash of the H.T.M. passes through LE MOTTES FM. at N.25.a.65.55. A H.T.M. has been reported previously from here.

At 12.30 a.m. an enemy patrol was seen at M.36.a.3.6. - it was dispersed by our fire. At 2.0 a.m. an enemy patrol was seen opposite MAUQUISSART CRATER at M.29.1. Two sentry groups opened fire and each claimed hits.

An enemy party in M.24.d. working on parapet was dispersed by our L.Gs. At 10. a.m. men passed breach at M.30.d.7.7. carrying sandbags. A man was seen carrying a large box at N.25. d.1.9.

Movement was seen behind screened road at N.25.d.9.5.

T.C.Heald

Head Qrs. 58th Divn.
7th January, 1917.
                Lieutenant,
        Intelligence, General Staff.

56th DIVISIONAL TACTICAL PROGRESS REPORT No. 73
from 8. 0 a.m. 7th January to 8. 0 a.m. 8th January, 1917.

On receipt of current copy of Divisional Tactical Progress Report
in the trenches, previous copy to be destroyed.

PART I OPERATIONS.

RIGHT SECTION.- Our artillery fired on enemy works near DISTILLERY and LES HOTTES FM. with good results. Our T Ms. fired on M.30.a.80.93 and on supposed M.G. at M.24.d.70.15. much debris was thrown into the air. Our patrols were again much hindered by the flooded state of the ground. The Craters at M.30.a.16.83. show no signs of enemy occupation and contain a considerable amount of water. One of our patrols endeavoured to enter the enemy trenches opposite M.24.2. but were prevented by wide ditches which they were unable to cross at about M.24.d.28.00. The enemy's wire here is low and thick. A hostile working party was observed about M.30.b.37.93. repairing the parapet. This was afterwards dispersed by L.G. fire.

LEFT SECTION.- Our artillery carried out a combined bombardment of houses at N.25.b.45.09., N.25.b.52.50 and the vicinity with good result. Our Trench Mortars fired on target at M.24.d.70.17. bombs were seen to burst well and considerable damage was done. The enemy did not retaliate. Our Machine Guns co-operated with the artillery shoot by indirect fire.

An Officers' patrol entered the enemy front line at DORA C.T. (N.24.d.9.6.) and inspected as far as N.19.c.22.92. In many places the trench is demolished. There is a concrete dugout intact at M.24.d.98.60. A machine gun emplacement which could still be used at N.19.c.15.80. snipers posts at the small saps N.19.c.05.75 and N.19.c.15.89. About 20 snipers plates many of the double pattern were seen along 200 yards of trench. Indicating DORA C.T. is a notice board lettered PREUSSEN GRABEN with arrow pointing down trench. The enemy wire is almost completely destroyed, but is stronger at N.19.c. 00.70.

Another Officers' patrol entered the German front line N. of RUE D'ENFER to bring in tramline and any other material. At the same time all the men in the Company who had not been on patrol were sent out to bring in iron pickets from the enemy wire in front of DEVIL'S JUMP. This party had just made their first journey back to our lines when the officers' patrol was fired on by a party of 8 Germans. It was thought that they had fired from some trees S. of RUE D'ENFER about 30 yards behind the front line. About half an hour later another patrol entered the German front line at N.19.a.3.7. turned to the right crossed the RUE D'ENFER and proceeded to the trees. The patrol found no sign of the enemy but several concrete dugouts full of water with loopholes for machine guns.

Another patrol entered the enemy's line at N.13.c.94.30. but found no signs of the enemy. A snipers plate, a pair of wire-cutters, and a number of screw pickets were brought back.

Another patrol entered the enemy's trench at N.14.c.10.70. but found nothing unusual.

Our aeroplanes were very active all day. One machine flying very low fired several bursts of machine gun fire into enemy trenches.

PART I INTELLIGENCE.

RIGHT SECTION.- Hostile artillery fired a few light shrapnel on one of our working parties, and later on to our communication trenches without doing any damage. Hostile T.Ms were quiet Our Lewis Guns dispersed two enemy working parties which had been located at M.30.a.80.55 and M.30.b.20.80.

/At

RIGHT SECTION (Contd.)
At 3.55 p.m. an enemy aeroplane flew over DUCKS BILL CRATER (M.36.a.00.00.) and dropped two small bombs. One fell on the lip of the Crater and the other missed, no damage was caused.

Two men were seen to leave the house at N.31.b.80.65. and walk to RUE DELEVAL at N.25.d.10.90. At M.30.c.50.90. there is a mound which may be a M.G.E. as several iron girders are visible. No Very lights were sent up opposite our extreme left during the night.

LEFT SECTION.- Hostile artillery and Trench Mortars were inactive.
A hostile Machine Gun is suspected to fire during the night from N.19.c.55.07. At N.15.c.15.90. movement and smoke was seen. Our artillery fired on this.

Movement was observed behind the Willows at N.20.b.30.35., in all 23 men were seen moving N.E. Usual movement was seen in AUBERS DEFENCES N.21.d.

A party of 10 men were seen on RUE DELEVAL N.14.d.8.4. moving towards the SUSA's HOUSE. Usual movement was seen on tracks at N.15.c.50.25. and N.21.a.8.8. our artillery chastised this.

Smoke was seen at N.20.b.25.42   ruins.
                   N.20.b.30.55   H.Q. dugout.
                   N.20.b.30.65   behind Willows
                   N.14.d.95.65.   dugout

Head Qrs. 56th Divn.
8th January, 1917.

Lieutenant,
Intelligence, General Staff.

56th DIVISIONAL TACTICAL PROGRESS REPORT No. 74
from 8.0 a.m January 8th to 8.0 a.m January 9th 1917.

On receipt of current copy of Divisional Tactical Progress Report
in the trenches, previous copy to be destroyed.

PART I OPERATIONS.

LEFT SECTION.- Our shelling dispersed several parties seen working in their back areas. Our T.Ms. fired on the C.T. at N.14.a.90.23. with the object of forming a block. Revetting material was thrown up and much damage was done. No retaliation. Our M.Gs. fired on to point N.14.c.30.10 during the night.

Patrol Patrols from our Right Company were unable to enter the enemy trench line S. of DORA C.T. as it was found to be in occupation and they were fired upon from the head of the C.T. and from M.24.d.6½.3. A strong patrol visited the clump of trees between TRIVELET and the German Front Line Trench from which last night's patrol suspected they were fired upon, no signs of the enemy were to be found. A patrol from our Centre Company selected a spot for a post at N.13.c.6.¼. an enemy patrol was sighted moving along the trench, our patrol law low in order not to draw attention to the spot selected. A patrol entered the centre of WICK SALIENT and examined ground 100 yards to Right and Left of it. They report WICK SALIENT to be flattened out by shell-fire, the whole area a morass, and that they could find no place for a post in it.

Seven out of nine patrols entered the enemy's line. Points N.14.a.75.25 and N.13.d.95.75 were found and thoroughly examined. Wire in front of them was cleared away and best way out from our lines to those points reconnoitred. The ground behind is still flooded and generally a foot of water over the mud in the trenches. The whole line was examined between point 120 yds. N. of IRMA to point 150 yds. S. of Crater N.13.d.95.75. A concrete dugout was found flooded at N.14.a.97.35. Close to this a hole suitable for T.M. Emplacement. Two open M.G. Emplacements are about 70 and 90 yards to N. of Crater. More bombs (of usual pattern) and a helmet were brought in. The ground in "NO MAN'S LAND" is still very bad.

RIGHT SECTION.- Our artillery bombarded EVA and FRIEDA C.Ts. and the enemy second line between M.30.d.45.50. and M.36.b.60.50. H.T.Ms. dealt with enemy mine shaft at M.30.c.50.55. whilst our other T.Ms. dealt with other targets near. Slight retaliation. Later, a few rounds fired at M.35.d.95.50. drew much retaliation.

Our patrols report that the enemy wire at M.36.a.40.90. is fairly thick and forms a good obstacle. No sign of enemy movement was discovered opposite M.35.3. trench, or opposite M.34.d.00.25.

Another patrol endeavoured to enter the enemy lines at M.30.a.40.15. They left 6 men at M.30.a.29.15. and 2 men at M.30.a.25.15. The Remainder advanced to a point just behind the slight ridge about 30 yards from the German trench and lay there for 30 minutes. The outline of the enemy parapet could be seen by the light of the moon, and two enemy sentry posts were located coughing being heard, also a man stamping to keep warm. The posts seemed about 40 yards apart. A man was heard walking along the duck-boards. Sentry posts located can be identified by day by reference to two tree stumps. Digging by about 2 men was heard at M.30.a.55.20. The parapet seemed very thick and to have suffered no serious damage from our fire. There is low wire 10 yards in front of the parapet.

P.T.O.

2.

PART II INTELLIGENCE.

LEFT SECTION. - The hostile artillery fired a few H.E. and Shrapnel on their own abandoned front line, and later on to our front line without doing any damage. Their T.Ms. were inactive.

A train was seen on the railway coming from the direction of AUBERS, and halting at N.27.b.32.30. Men were seen to unload trucks.

A small patrol from the Corps on our left who remained in the German line N.8.d.7.2. during daylight report that 5 dead Germans were found lying in the trench. They located a M.G. Emplacement at N.14.b.6.6. The tripod being plainly visible. Also 50 yards S.W. of this position 2 Germans were seen peeping from behind a mound. A platform was seen in a tree at N.15.a.5.2. thought to be an O.P. Considerable movement was observed yesterday on the road in N.21.b, timber being carried from the dump at N.21.b.35.15. Our artillery fired on several occasions, once causing three casualties, 3 men appearing three minutes later, 2 with head bandaged & one apparently wounded in the arm.

The usual sentry and movement were seen in MOSSY TRENCH the sentry fired 2 rounds with his rifle afterwards scanning our line with his field glasses. Work continues on the new trench from N.26.c. to N.32.a. also on trench at N.27.a.94.90. A dugout resembling our elephant iron structure is visible at N.26.d.7.8. Much movement was observed yesterday on RUE DELEVAL in N.14.d. A working party of about 30 men were seen digging in a field at N.25.d.60.60. Movement was also seen on the tracks in N.15.c. Smoke was seen N.15.c.40.20. dugouts
N.20.a.87.63.
N.20.b.30.55. H.Q. dugout.
N.14.d.00.03 MOSSY TRENCH.
N.21.d.90.10. Trench

There are two sentries plainly visible in BERTHA TRENCH near its junction with the RUE DELEVAL.

RIGHT SECTION.- Hostile artillery retaliated to our bombardment with a few shells which fell near MOATED GRANGE and Front Line at M.30.1. Hostile T.Ms. were quiet. A hostile M.G. is suspected to be firing from the DISTILLERY - N.19.c.5.0.

Enemy working parties were heard last night about M.30.a.55.20. and M.30.b.4.9. New work is reported at M.30.c.55.85. Several men were seen near M.30.d.70.80. carrying rifles. Movement was seen at the Cross Roads N.25.b.35.20. Two men were seen working on EVA C.T. at N.25.c.7.1. twenty men in all wearing steel helmets and greatcoats were seen moving along the road from N.32.d.2.8. to T.2.b. Two German Officers were seen near the dump at N.25.b.0.9. At N.31.b.2.8. a working party of about 12 men were seen walking along on the top of the trench, they disappeared behind the trees at N.31.b.2.4.

At M.30.d.65.80. there is a large mound suggesting a M.G.E.

Smoke was seen at trench M.30.a.60.30 and chimney at N.25.b.5.1.

Head Qrs. 56th Divn.
9th January, 1917.

Lieutenant,
Intelligence, General Staff.

56th DIVISIONAL TACTICAL PROGRESS REPORT No. 75
from 8.0 a.m 9th January, to 8.0 a.m. 10th January 1917.

On receipt of current copy of Divisional Tactical Progress Report
in the trenches, previous copy to be destroyed.

PART I OPERATIONS.

RIGHT SECTION.- Our artillery confined themselves to retaliation for enemy's shelling and chastisement of enemy working parties.
Our patrols covered our front during the night but could find no signs of the enemy. Our wire from M.35.b.95.05. to M.35.b.95.90. is reported to have been damaged.
Our snipers had several targets in the course of the day and claimed two victims at M.30.c.35.10

LEFT SECTION.- Between 2.0 p.m. and 2.45 p.m. our artillery and T.Ms. carried out an organised shoot on enemy strong points at N.19.a.60.65. and N.19.c.04.48. Much damage was done and much boarding was seen in the air. Enemy retaliation was slight and did no damage. During the night our Machine Guns fired on to enemy H.Q. at N.21.a.6.6.
At dusk an Officers' patrol attempted to enter the German lines N. of its junction with DORA C.T. in order to work down to that point and establish an ambush there. They tried to get over the ditches lying across their front between TRIVELET and DORA C.T. but failed to do so. It was impossible to avoid much splashing which attracted hostile attention. The enemy appear to hold the head of DORA c.t. permanently and not to have evacuated it.
The first steps towards the consolidation by us of the abandoned German line were taken last night. Four permanent posts were successfully established at the following places,: viz :-(1)N.13.c.60.00 in a line of shell holes along the parapet. This post has a good field of fire and considerable work was done on it. (2) N.13.d.8.6. the position is not good, but it is the best available on account of the damaged condition of the trenches and the flooded state of the ground. (3) N.13.d.95.75 the head of BERTHA C.T. - all these posts were occupied by 6.45 p.m. - and (4) N.14.a.8.25. the head of IRMA C.T. It was impossible to ger into this post until 6.15 a.m. owing to a strong hostile patrol being in occupation with a machine gun, although three attemps were made during the night. Seven other patrols were out during the night but had nothing further to report. The Division on our Left report that the enemy's front line on their extreme right is unoccupied. Our snipers claimed to have hit a man carrying a plank about 12' long at N.14.c.08.53. Two shots were fired and he was seen to fall.

PART II INTELLIGENCE.

RIGHT SECTION.- Hostile artillery and T.Ms. were quiet, except for a few light shells falling on M.35.4. and M.29 central. A few rifle grandes were fired at DUCK'S BILL CRATER M.36.a.0.0. but no damage was done. An enemy working party was heard for a short time about M.30.c.5.6. Two Germans were seen laying wire at N.32.a.30.95. and were fired on. Two hostile working parties seen at N.33.c.00.40. and N.32.c.5.5. were dispersed by our artillery.

LEFT SECTION.- Hostile artillery fired a few shells chiefly 4.2" along our front line during the afternoon. The hostile M.G. mentioned above firing from the junction of IRMA C.T. and the front line fired bursts from 12.15 a.m. to 5.30 a.m. on to our front line.
Small enemy working parties seen in N.15.c. at intervals during the day were dispersed by our artillery. A hostile

/working

working party was seen at N.32.a.80.30 erecting wire on the new trench. At N.21.d.22.10. new work is visible thought to be a dugout in course of construction.

New work has been observed in the enemy front line trench at its junction with DORA C.T. and at the DEVIL'S JUMP. At the former spot the parapet has been raised and fresh sandbags and revetting stakes can be seen. At the latter spot (DEVIL'S JUMP) new sheets of corrugated iron and fresh woodwork are visible.

At 2.30 p.m. earth was being thrown over the parapet about N.14.a.95.09. A cart is visible on RUE DELEVAL at N.14.b.95.40. forming a barricade. There is a permanent sentry post in the QUADRILATERAL at N.25.b.8.9. and smoke has been observed rising from this spot. A large number of telephone wires running to the house at N.20.d.50.85. What looked like gun-pits can be seen N. of RUE DELEVAL at N.20.c.4.8. At 11.15 a.m. water was seen to be pumped out of trench at N.26.a.80.20.

Smoke was seen at :-

N.14.d.90.65	house.
N.14.c.15.57	dugout.
N.20.b.30.55	H.Q. dugout.
N.21.d.3.1.	AUBERS DEFENCES
N.22.c. 32.34	do.

Head Qrs. 53th Divn.
10th January, 1917.

Lieutenant,
Intelligence, General Staff.

56th DIVISIONAL TACTICAL PROGRESS REPORT No. 76.
from 8. 0 a.m 10th January to 8. 0 a.m 11th January, 1917.

On receipt of current copy of Divisional Tactical Progress Report in the trenches, previous copy to be destroyed.

PART I OPERATIONS.

RIGHT SECTION.- At 11. a.m and 2. p.m. our Trench Mortars fired on to the enemy front line at M.36.a. 4.7. He retaliated with aerial torpedoes and shrapnel which seems to point to the fact that a tender spot was touched. Our M.Gs. traversed strong point N.25. b.50.10. to point N.25.c.50.70. with indirect fire.

One of our patrols entered the enemy trenches at M.24.d.40.05. They found the trench badly damaged and dugouts wrecked. There was a derelict truck on the railway just behind. Work was heard to the left, and about 60 yards up the railway line to the rear. Another patrol examined the wire in front of the Craters about M.30.a.5.6. this was in good order and some new wire had been recently put out. Other patrols were out but report no signs of enemy. Our snipers fired on a party passing the house at M.36.b.1.7. at 11.40 a.m. result not observed.

LEFT SECTION.- During the day an organised shoot in three phases was carried out by our Howitzers, Field Guns and H.T.Ms. against the enemy's strong point at N.14.b.25.30. and N.14.d.3.9. and in an endeavour to flood IRMA C.T. The shoot was very successful. Our artillery also dispersed working parties at N.21.d.30.50. N.22.c.70.50. N.21.a.90.70. N.20.a.77.63. and N.32.a.80.30.

During the night our Machine Guns fired on to points N.14.b. 50.20 and surrounding area. This produces retaliation by enemy field guns which searched for our Machine Guns. During the night a patrol visited the DEVIL'S JUMP for the purpose of selecting a site for a new post and report that post will have to be placed in shell holes in front of the parapet. Whilst the patrol was out a German patrol approached, they lay in wait for it and shot two men. The remaining two ran away, one appeared to be wounded. Patrol was unable to get to the bodies. Shortly afterwards at 1.30 a.m. enemy's artillery, T.Ms. and M.Gs. opened fire on the area between the french lines. This bombardment ceased at 2.15 a.m. At its height there were about 5 shells per minute. A patrol reconnoitred the ground from post at N.13.c. 60.10. Northward to WICK SALIENT, looking for a site to which to move post now at N.13.d.80.80. They report that they could find nothing suitable, confirming report of daylight patrol and patrols of previous nights.

IRMA POST reports hearing enemy working on communication trench about 50 yards away. Every time one of our H.T.Ms. was fired they heard a working party dropping shovels and running along the duck-boards. H.T.Ms. were well directed. Patrols during the night visited all the posts and patrolled the ground between, but found nothing special to report.

PART II INTELLIGENCE.

RIGHT SECTION.- The enemy artillery showed some activity yesterday firing chiefly on to our support and reserve lines, little damage was done. Hostile T.Ms. fired a few rounds on to M.35.b.7.8. doing no damage. A hostile machine gun suspected to fire from M.36.a.45.50.

At 11.20 a.m. two small motor lorries were seen at N.25.c.9.6. Working parties were seen at M.36.b.60.15., M.30.b.2.8. and M.30.a.3.4. and were dispersed by L.G. fire. A new sandbag revetment can be seen at M.36.a.45.40. There is a suspected tree O.P. at M.30.a.47.65. Several times during the day thick white smoke and flame were observed at M.36.b.3.7.
GRETCHEN C.T. There is a suspected O.P. at N.31.b.94.20.

/LEFT SECTION.

LEFT SECTION.- The enemy's retaliation to our shoot was practically nil, a few shells falling on the PICANTIN C.T. about N.8.c.2.6. Between 1.10 and 3.0 p.m. smoke from trains approaching and leaving AUBERS was seen.

A considerable amount of new work has appeared in the German trenches S. of TRIVELET since yesterday. In front of DORA C.T. about 100 yards of new wire apparently a single apron fence can be seen. In DORA C.T. there are further signs of new work, and at two points on the front line between that trench and TRIVELET. At the T.M. Emplacement at N.14.c.25.65. black screens have been taken out and replaced by light coloured ones. Two black boards or boxes about 2 ft. square are visible in the trees at M.14.d.12.80. and N.14.d.20.88. Close to the former tree there appears to be a dugout from which smoke was seen.

Three men were seen to enter the house on the RUE D'ENFER close to the DISTILLERY. At 1.30 p.m. two men with field glasses entered the house at N.25.b.80.90. and observed from the roof a few minutes later. Movement on LA CLIQUETERIE FM. Rd. in T.3.a. was rather above the usual.

Smoke was seen at :-

N.20.b.1.4.	dugout.
N.20.a.82.73.	disused trench.
N.26.c.15.83.	house.
N.21.d.40.15.	AUBERS DEFENCES.
N.26.d.05.80.	do.
N.22.c.65.60.	FROMELLES

and several house in AUBERS.

Head Qrs. 53th Divn.
11th January, 1917.

Lieutenant,
Intelligence, General Staff.

56th DIVISIONAL TACTICAL PROGRESS REPORT No. 77
from 8.0 a.m. 11th January to 8.0 a.m. 12th January, 1917.

On receipt of current copy of Divisional Tactical Progress Report in the trenches, previous copy to be destroyed.

PART I. OPERATIONS.

RIGHT SECTION. Our Artillery and Heavy Trench Mortars carried out a very successful shoot on M.30.b.30.30. and M.24.d.65.15. Much damage was done. Retaliation considerable. Our Machine guns sprayed the enemy's communications during the night. The patrol which entered the enemy's trenches at M.24.d 40.05, reported in yesterday's summary further reported that the craters at M.30.a.65.65 were surrounded by barbed and French wire recently put up, the dyke at M.30.a.8.7. was five feet deep and would need a bridge 12 feet long to cross it, 5" pipes were found leading out of dugout in the enemy's line, the derelict railway truck contained cement slabs and the general mode of construction of the German trench is similar to our own. Our patrols last night could not find any signs of the enemy, they were greatly hampered by the extreme darkness. Enemy's Very lights were falling behind the craters at M.30.a.5.4.

Our snipers fired at a periscope at about M.24.d.6.2.. It was removed.

LEFT SECTION. Our Artillery carried out two organised shoots on CLARA and DORA C.T. satisfactory results being obtained. Our trench mortars co-operated in this. Enemy did not retaliate.

Soon after 5 p.m. one of our Stokes mortars was taken out to a position at N.19.a.00.60. for barrage fire required. It returned at 6 a.m. not having fired. Our Machine Guns displayed their usual activity.

One of our patrols entered the German lines S. of DORA C.T. and worked N., they found Germans in the trench and threw two bombs amongst them. At that moment our Machine Guns from the rear opened overhead fire and our patrol had to fall back. This patrol constantly sniped the garrison on DORA C.T. and prevented them working on their wire. A position was selected in the German front line trench close to the southern edge of the RUE D'ENFER for establishing a post tonight. Repeated attempts were made to establish a post at DEVILS JUMP. A party went out at 5.10 p.m. only to find the enemy in position. It was several times reconnoitred during the night and at 6.10 a.m. this morning enemy were reported to be still working there and pumping water. It is considered that a post could be established tonight at N.19.a.30.50. Close to BERTHA Post (N.13.d.95.75.) two concrete dugouts and a mine shaft were found all flooded. The mine shaft had a notice board with the word "MUNCHEN" painted on it fixed to the shaft house. No place was found suitable for a post in the SUGAR LOAF. Our patrols kept in touch along the German parapet. About 30 yards of the northern end of IRMA C.T. can be seen by day and the water in the trench appears to be about 4 feet deep.

PART II. INTELLIGENCE.

RIGHT SECTION. The hostile Artillery and Trench Mortars were quiet. A hostile machine gun was firing from the direction of DORA C.T.

No Very lights were fired from the enemy trenches opposite our extreme left. Observation was difficult during the day owing to mist.

LEFT SECTION. Hostile Artillery and Trench Mortars were inactive, except for a few light shells which fell on our support lines during the afternoon. During the morning hostile machine gun was firing from CLARA C.T. about N.19.a.80.40. A hostile patrol of four was seen in front of BERTHA Post but quickly disappeared going S. Our post at N.13.c.60.10. reported sounds of work - hammering and pumping at DEVILS JUMP during the night. New earth was observed to be thrown up at N.20.a.77.63. Between 1.30 and 2.30 p.m. several men were seen carrying timber from the dump at N.21.b.35.15. and walking along the road in a S.W. direction. At 3.0 p.m. much smoke was seen to rise from hedge at N.21.d.9.4. Four men were seen at N.21.d.2.1. on the road walking N.E.

Hdqrs. 56th Divn.
12th January, 1917.

Lieut. for Captain,
Intelligence, General Staff.

56th DIVISIONAL TACTICAL PROGRESS REPORT No. 78
from 8. 0 a.m. January 12th to 8. 0 a.m. January 13th 1917.

On receipt of current copy of Divisional Tactical Progress Report
in the trenches, previous copy to be destroyed.

PART I OPERATIONS.

RIGHT SECTION.- Our artillery and T.Ms. co-operated in bombarding the enemy trenche junctions, dugouts and RUE DU PIETRE in M.30. The result was again very successful, much material being thrown up into the air. Our M.Gs. were active with indirect fire on to the enemy's communications during the night.

Our patrols examined the ditches in front of M.35.4. they averaged from three to six feet wide and two to four feet deep. Another patrol examined the ditch at M.30...c.1.2. which in parts was impassable, being 10 yards wide and 5 ft. deep. Other patrols reported work heard in the enemy trench about M.36.a.30.32., the wire from M.24.d.5.1. towards DORA C.T. to be very thick, sounds of pumping were heard in M.24.d.50.15. and DORA C.T., the dyke at M.30.c.10.95. can be crossed by means of a plank at M.30.a.20.01., sounds of movement and coughing were heard at M.30.a.41.15., there is a gap in the wire at M.30.a.4.0.

LEFT SECTION.- Between 3 and 5.15 p.m. our artillery and T.Ms. co-operated in a shoot on the enemy lines with the idea of preparing the way for two additional posts to be established in the enemy's abandoned front line, the chief targets being N.1.a.58.37. and 34.36. Much damage was done. The enemy retaliated with about 20 rounds of H.E. shrapnel which mostly burst in front of the parapet.

At 6.30 p.m. one of our Stokes Mortars and crew took up a position at N.19.a.1.5. to cover a post in case of need.. Immediately our bombardment ceased the new posts were established - one which it is proposed to name ENFIELD POST at N.19.a.45.80. and the other proposed name HAMPSTEAD HEATH at N.19.a.30.30. The presence of the latter post was discovered by the enemy about 12.30 a.m. when a Very light went up, three bombs were thrown and later a few shells bursts near the post. Both posts report that the ground was badly cut up by our artillery fire and the site originally selected for HAMPSTEAD HEATH POST was so damaged that the post had to be moved a little further away. Our patrols report that the enemy appear to be working hard at the head of DORA and CLARA C.Ts. The enemy's line between IRMA and SUGAR LOAF was carefully examined by us. A supposed wiring party was seen North of SUGAR LOAF but was dealt with by a New Zealand patrol. Movement was heard behind the front line but it was impossible to get across the tramline owing to water which is more than waist deep. The water is rising again and IR A C.T. is in a very bad state. At about N.14.a.80.40. is a concrete dugout partly blown in but roof intact. A machine gun was located about N.14.b.6.20. BERTHA C.T. has no apparent junction with "our" front line, the water is 20 to 30 yards wide. No one can approach our post from the enemy's side without being seen. An artillery test message from WICK post wired at 8.56 p.m. Shell arrived at 8.56.30 p.m. Patrolling of the new NO MAN'S LAND is now very difficult owing to mud and water.

PART II INTELLIGENCE.

RIGHT SECTION.- The hostile artillery were intermittently active.
Targets - reserve line - front line left and GREAT EASTERN RAILWAY.
A few light T.Ms. fell around M.24.1. but no damage was caused.
A hostile patrol was heard about M.30.a.3.8. but could not be traced. Sounds of hammering were heard about M.30.b.4.9. and digging at M.36.d.45.50. Two Germans were seen wearing dark blue uniform. The enemy were using white-green and white-red and two white lights last evening. No action was noticed.

/LEFT SECTION.

2.

LEFT SECTION.- Hostile artillery and T.Ms. were quiet except as mentioned above. Hostile machine guns fired several bursts during the night from some distance back in BERTHA C.T. and believed also from N.14.b. 6.2. Several hostile patrols were seen, viz:- One at 3.30 a.m. opposite our WICK POST estimated at 20 strong, but did not approach near enough to be dealt with. Shortly after this patrol retired hurriedly. During the relief of BERTHA POST a hostile patrol was seen behind the swamp on the farther side of the RIV. des LAIES. Also some bombs were thrown at our post at N.19.a.3.3. Movement was seen in BERTHA C.T., in rear of 14 TREE CLUMP, on track at N.21.a.9.7., RUE DELEVAL, and LE PLUME.
Two men were seen repairing the parapet about N.20.b.35.39.
A dugout is suspected at N.20.b.25.50. Five men were seen to leave this spot, moving South, and smoke was also seen. Four men observed carrying small wooden boxes from LE CLERCQ F&E. N.27.b.7.8. along track to N.21.d.40.15. where they dumped them.

Smoke seen at :-
    N.20.a.82.73.   disused trench, reported yesterday.
    N.20.b.20.45   house.
    N.21.a.60.50   "
    N.27.c.30.99.   ruins.
    N.27.a.20.20.   dugouts.

At 4.30 p.m. a red light was seen in the air behind AUBERS at about N.27.c.28.80.

Lieutenant,
Intelligence, General Staff.

Head Qrs. 56th Divn.
13th January, 1917.

56th DIVISIONAL TACTICAL PROGRESS REPORT No. 79;
from 8.0 a.m. 13th Jany. to 8.0 a.m., 14th January, 1917.

On receipt of current copy of Divisional Tactical Progress Report
in the trenches, previous copy to be destroyed.

PART I OPERATIONS.

RIGHT SECTION. Our Artillery fired in retaliation and on working parties during the day. A shoot was carried out on the MOULIN du PIETRE - BAS POMMEREAU Road. Our trench mortars fired on the enemy rifle grenade position M.36.a.35.15. No grenades have since been fired from here. We also fired on the trench mortar emplacement M.35.a.8.5 ; much damage was caused and a big explosion took place. For the first time the enemy failed to reply with his trench mortars against our activity. Our patrols were active over the whole front. A patrol of 2 officers and 28 other ranks moved to the German line which was entered at M.24.d.5 1 Path was taped and bridges placed across ditches in NO MANS LAND. Sentry groups were posted around the point of entry and a small patrol pushed out in each direction into the German line, penetrated for 150 yards, and found no signs of the enemy. After spending nearly four hours in the German trenches the patrol returned. The German lines are in a bad condition. The support line, about 40 yards back, was in an even worse condition than the front line. A mine shaft was discovered at point of entry in a fairly good state of repair, but flooded. There is a dug-out with pumping apparatus about 50 yards from the mine shaft and a water pipe and an air pipe leading out and telephone wires attached. A C.T. running S.E. from 15 yards S. of the point of entry was completely flooded. Very lights were being fired from far in rear of the front line. The craters in M.30.a. were reconnoitred with a view to establishing post. Suitable position was selected and guide wires laid to it. It was also hoped to use a Stokes gun from the craters, but ground was everywhere much too soft to allow this. Enemy wire was examined from M.36.a.31.90. to M.30.c.5.3. It is thick and fairly new in parts. Our patrols attempted to approach the crater at M.30.a.24.20. were observed and fired upon.

LEFT SECTION. Our Artillery carried out registration on the new S.O.S. lines. Otherwise very quiet. The relief of the five Northern posts in the German front line were carried out without incident, but at 6.0 p.m. the post at N.19.a. .3.3. was rushed by a party of enemy estimated at 50. They were not seen until quite close to the post. The Lewis gun jammed and men were so stiff with cold that they could not make adequate resistance. One man is missing. An attempt was made to re-establish this post on the Northern side of the RUE d'ENFER about N.19.a.5.3., but the enemy were found in position here. They were working hard all night and were still there at daybreak. Patrols kept in touch with enemy line at head of DORA trench; it was still held at daybreak by enemy.

PART II INTELLIGENCE.

RIGHT SECTION. There was some shrapnel over the left battalion area at dusk. A few light and medium trench mortar bombs fell near the front line in M.35.b. and towards S.E. railhead. No damage was caused. Hostile machine guns were firing from the direction of LES MOTTES Farm. Working parties were heard behind the craters in M.30.a. at a considerable distance Right battalion patrols report an exceptional amount of talking in the enemy lines, general quietness of artillery and suggest a relief in progress. There was some movement on the BAS POMMEREAU Road this morning.

LEFT SECTION. Hostile Artillery slightly more active in the morning. Some field gun shells on M.24. 5 and 6 and near CONVENT O.P. About 20 rounds 4.2" distributed about N.7.d. A fresh line of wire has been put out running from front line trench at M.24.d.75.40. to support line M.19.c.1.5. A few men were seen during the day moving timber and some boxes from the dump N.21.b.35.15. Usual movement was observed on the tracks N.15.c. and 21.a. Smoke from the
        house N.20.b.30.30.
  front line M.36.a.4.9.
    dump N.21.b.35.15

Hdqrs. 56th Divn.
14th January, 1917

Captain,

56th DIVISIONAL TACTICAL PROGRESS REPORT No. 80.
from 8.0 a.m. 14th January to 8.0 a.m. 15th January, 1917.

On receipt of current copy of Divisional Tactical Progress Report
in the trenches, previous copy to be destroyed.

PART I OPERATIONS.

RIGHT SECTION.- A Trench Mortar bombardment was carried out on the enemy
line M.30.c.5.6.   Divisional Artillery co-operated on GRETCHEN &
FRIEDA TRENCHES and MIN DU PIETRE.   Mist made observation difficult.
Yesterday working party was dispersed during
the bombardment, and gaps have been cut in the enemy wire by M.T.Ms.
at M.30.a.50.05 & M.30.c.56.60.   Much damage was caused to the enemy
line at M.36.a.4.7.   Enemy retaliated with 4.2"s.

Our machine guns were active in the early part of the night on
enemy's communications.

A patrol visited M.24.d.5.1.where a post had been previously
occupied, and reports no signs of the enemy.   Another patrol reports
wire from M.30.a.4.2. to M.30.c.5.6. badly damaged and several gaps
made.   Movement could be heard in the enemy trenches here and patrol
was fired on.   Enemy wire was examined at M.36.a.3.3. to M.36.a.32.57
and wire reported thick.   Enemy could be heard in trench M.36.a.32.30
walking up and down.   Enemy patrol was seen at M.35.b.95.55. and fired
upon and driven into their lines.

LEFT SECTION.- From 4 to 6 p.m. our guns fired on their night lines round
posts in the enemy lines, and it is believed that casualties were
inflicted. Between 3 and 4.30 p.m. T.Ms. carried out fire against
TRIVELET FM.   Our snipers claim a hit.

In the fog yesterday morning at 9.30 a party of 25 Germans rushed
BERTHA POST N.13.d.97.74 - 1 Officer and 4 Other ranks were killed,
and 1 Officer and   5 Other ranks missing.   At 10.30 a.m. patrol
re-entered the POST and found the enemy had again evacuated it.   This
was re-established at noon in spite of enemy rifle fire.   A party of
about 10 Germans which came over the open towards POST were dispersed
by rifle fire.

PART II INTELLIGENCE.

RIGHT SECTION.- Hostile artillery was more active than usual with 4.2" A
direct hit was obtained on M.29.2. otherwise no damage.   A few T.Ms.
fell towards MOATED GRANGE.
Visibility was poor throughout the day.

LEFT SECTION.- A few rounds of shrapnel shells fell on our support line
in the Left Sub-section.   There was no T.M. fire during the period.
Two machine guns fired from the enemy second line in the evening -
one gun appeared to be near the SUGAR LOAF, and one about N.14.c.6.2.
Two pumps were working without ceasing in the German line opposite
WICK POST.

Head Qrs. 56th Divn.
15th January, 1917.

Captain,
Intelligence, General Staff.

56th DIVISIONAL TACTICAL PROGRESS REPORT No. 61.
from 8.0 a.m. 15th January to 8.0 a.m. 16th January, 1917.

On receipt of current copy of Divisional Tactical Progress Report in the trenches, previous copy to be destroyed.

PART I OPERATIONS.

RIGHT SECTION. Our Artillery and Heavy Trench Mortars confined themselves to a few rounds for registration purposes. Our Machine guns showed their usual activity during the night. One of our patrols examined the enemy wire from M.30.c.50.75 to salient at M.30.a.40.15. Sounds of talking were heard at the latter spot. Later, another patrol visited this salient and threw bombs into the enemy trench with the object of getting a definite location of a hostile post. There was no reply. Another patrol reconnoitred the enemy's wire at M.30.c.5.6. They threw bombs into the enemy trench at this point but failed to draw fire. Another patrol entered the enemy trenches at M.24.d.45.10. They discovered a mine shaft at M.24.d.40.00. and a deep dugout at M.24.d.55.20. The trenches are very derelict generally, water everywhere being about 3' deep, but these posts which have not been destroyed are well revetted and good fire steps exist. A specimen of wire leading to the dugout, a chart found in a trench, and a specimen of the enemy's barbed wire were brought in. Another patrol examined the mine crater at M.30.a.50.65. Nothing was seen or heard of the enemy. Very lights seen to be sent up about 200 yards to the rear. Our snipers claim two victims yesterday, one in GRETCHEN C.T. and the other at M.24.d.55.10.

LEFT SECTION. Our Artillery were quiet, except for registration, but our machine guns kept up an intermittent fire on to enemy C.T's., tracks and drains along which our posts could be approached. Our patrols were out all night visiting our posts at frequent intervals and the trenches between were thoroughly examined. About 50 yards N. of BERTHA Post a cupboard containing 40 German bombs in good condition was found. These were thrown into the water. The trench at this point is duck boarded and the water about 2'6" deep. The old German trench about N.8.c.4.3. was examined but nothing was seen or heard of the enemy. A body of a German Unter-officier was found close to BERTHA Post. One of our patrols went out to find the position of the enemy post near TRIVELET. They located the enemy post at N.19.a.3.1. where they definitely heard foreign voices and sounds of work going on. They estimated the number of men at about 24. The trench seemed deserted on either side. This patrol then proceeded to the point where the trench cuts the road at N.19.a.30.35. They listened here and heard sounds like the butt of a rifle being tapped on the fire step. They also heard sounds of subdued coughing. They concluded that this was a detached sentry from the post ready to give alarm in case of attack. They then retired and approached the line again at N.19.c.1.7., but could hear no signs of enemy occupation here.

PART II INTELLIGENCE.

RIGHT SECTION. Hostile Artillery fired a few small H.E. shells on to M.29.d.9.8. Hostile trench mortars and machine guns were quiet. A small enemy working party was seen in the enemy front line opposite M.35.4. trench. It was dispersed by our Artillery.

LEFT SECTION. Hostile Artillery and Trench Mortars very inactive, but their machine guns fired intermittently throughout the day and night over the old NO MANS LAND. A little movement was observed on the usual tracks in N.21.a. At 3.0 p.m., a working party was seen in MOSSY Trench at N.20.b.05.95. Our Artillery fired on this target. Papers taken from the body of the German Unter-officier, killed at BERTHA Post yesterday, show that he belongs to the 19th Bavarian Infantry Regiment (normal Order of Battle) He appeared to have been hit in the chest by a bullet.

Hdqrs. 56th Divn.
16th January, 1917.

Lieut. for Captain,
Intelligence, General Staff.

56th DIVISIONAL TACTICAL PROGRESS REPORT No. 82
from 8.0 a.m. 16th January to 8.0 a.m. 17th January 1917.

On receipt of current copy of Divisional Tactical Progress Report
in the trenches, previous copy to be destroyed.

PART I OPERATIONS.

RIGHT SECTION. – Our artillery and T.Ms. combined in an offensive shoot on the enemy's trenches from M.30.a.75.00. to M.30.d.00.35. Our T.Ms. paying special attention to the enemy wire at M.30.c.50.70 Direct hits were obtained and much damage was done. One of our patrols inspected the enemy wire at M.30.a.90.60. The wire is close up to the parapet and does not appear strong. Talking and sounds of wooden stakes being driven with a maul were heard approximately at M.30.a.90.45. The Craters in M.30.a. were examined and found unoccupied. A sniper was active from about M.30.a.60.28. At 5.45 p.m. a patrol consisting of 1 officer and 20 other ranks proceeded to the enemy wire at M.30.c.50.60. When about 50 yards from the enemy parapet an order was heard to be given and 5 rifles opened fire on the patrol. As the wire at this point is strong there was no possibility of rushing the post. The rifle fire continued intermittently for 25 minutes so the patrol withdrew. A Machine Gun opened fire from the second line at about M.30.a.70.00. Another patrol of 1 Officer and 7 Other ranks reconnoitred the same place at 2 a.m. The enemy wire at M.30.c. 55.75. was much damaged. Patrol then moved South to enemy wire at M.30.c.52.60. After passing through the wire here they were immediately fired upon, the Officer being killed. Very Lights were sent up and two parties estimated at about 15 each could be seen leaving enemy trench 1 on either side of patrol. The Sergeant after carefully examining the body ordered the patrol to withdraw. It was impossible to bring in the body. The Officer was wearing badges of the Monmouth Regiment and no other identification marks.

LEFT SECTION. – Our artillery carried out a Group Programme during the afternoon firing on road and trench junction along RUE DELEVAL. Enemy working parties were dispersed at N.21.a.9.9. and at N.26.c. 8.2. where 3 casualties were observed. Our M.Gs. fired down the C.Ts. in the old German system leading up to our posts.

The portions of the old German line between our Posts was patrolled but no signs of the enemy could be found. A suitable site to establish a new post on the extreme right of DEVIL'S JUMP could not be found. One of our patrols reconnoitred BERTHA C.T. as far as the River LAIES. BERTHA C.T. was flooded and could be seen continuing on the other side of the river, but nothing could be found of the bridge except a number of stakes standing in the water. In trying to ascertain the depth of the river they made a noise breaking the ice. This was evidently heard by the enemy in a trench close to the further side of the river. The patrol could distinctly hear hurried movement as of 8 or 10 men moving excitedly and a bomb was thrown at the patrol from the enemy side of the river but it fell into the water. The patrol then turned back towards BERTHA POST and heard sounds as if three men were moving through the trench at M.14.c.00.55. which runs into BERTHA C.T. They examined the spot but no enemy were located.

Another patrol reconnoitred IRMA C.T. for a hundred yards moving at a distance of 80 yards to the left of the C.T. Upon reaching M.14.a.90.25. they were challenged in German. Patrol halted and located two enemy parties each 12 strong which appeared to be standing patrols. The two parties were about 20 yards apart. Our patrol withdrew slowly to IRMA POST and warned the garrison to stand to. The enemy parties did not follow or fire upon the patrol. The ground is covered with shell holes and in parts practically impassable.

P.T.O.   /PART II INTELLIGENCE.

PART II INTELLIGENCE.

RIGHT SECTION.- Hostile artillery fired chiefly on to our C.Ts. About 12 L.T.Ms. were fired on to our right front but caused no damage. There are some new sandbags to be seen in the mound at M.30.c.30.41. At about 1.15 p.m. two men were observed on the screened road at N.25.d.10.85.

LEFT SECTION.- Hostile artillery fired over our C.Ts. and the RUE TILLELOY during the afternoon apparently in reply to our fire over RUE DELEVAL.

A man was seen throwing up earth at about N.19.b.35.60.

An enemy patrol about 5 in all were seen approaching BERTHA POST last night at 5.15 p.m. rifle fire was opened and rifle grenades were fired from BERTHA and FLAME POST. and patrol disappeared immediately. The enemy appeared nervous early last night. At 4.45 p.m. 1 red and 1 Green rocket were sent up. The only result seemed to be that bombs were thrown up from the Posts half right and half left of HIGH BARNET (N.13.c.60.02.) and 400 yards away where work was observed. Shortly afterwards 5 red, green and white rockets went up from a point further right, and the enemy threw bombs from about N.19.a.3.1. the post which was located the night before.

Usual movement was observed on the AUBERS DEFENCES at M.21.d. Also on the tracks in N.21.a. Our artillery dealt with these.

A few men were observed around the dump at N.21.b.30.15.

Head Qrs. 55th Divn.
17th January, 1917.

Lieutenant,
Intelligence, General Staff.

56th DIVISIONAL TACTICAL PROGRESS REPORT No. 83
from 8.0 a.m. 17th January, 1917 to 8.0 a.m. 18th Jany. 1917.

On receipt of current copy of Divisional Tactical Progress Report
in the trenches, previous copy to be destroyed.

PART I OPERATIONS.

RIGHT SECTION. Our Artillery carried out night firing on trenches about M.36.a.65.25., GRETCHEN Trench and M.36 a 40.90. to 50.20. Our trench mortars fired on enemy post at M.30.c.50 60., several direct hits being obtained. One of our patrols examined the road running N.E. in M.35.d. The road is broad and flooded; the water being about four feet deep. Very lights were sent up from approx. M.36 c.05.60. and sounds of movement were heard. The enemy wire appears strong, and is about 40 yards from the parapet. Another patrol attempted to find the body of the officer killed last night but failed to do so. A few shots were fired from the salient at M.30.c.50.60., but not intended for patrol. The BIRDCAGE Craters in M.30.c. were thoroughly examined. The trench at M.30.a.86.56. is flooded. Enemy working parties were heard at about M.30.a.64.35. and 55.15. The enemy's wire at M.30.a 90.55. is thick, but a few gaps exist about M.30.a.45.45. The enemy seems suspicious and several Very lights were fired towards the patrol. Another patrol which tried to approach M.30.a. 50.30. was fired on: quiet progress was difficult. Coughing and low voices were heard in the trench.

LEFT SECTION. Our Artillery fired intermittently on to the enemy C.Ts. during the afternoon: many direct hits were observed, whilst our machine guns sprayed these places during the night. One of our patrols made a thorough reconnaissance of the hostile post on EERTHA C.T. located last night on far side of the river. Enemy post is about N.14.c.15.36. Four men were seen at one time and two sentries were visible. Digging and movement were heard but patrol could not get within bombing distance owing to the width of the river. The trench was too full of water to move in so they proceeded parallel to it at a distance of 40 yards to the right. The ground was very cut up and going difficult and the ditch they had to cross before reaching the river LAIES presented a considerable obstacle. On reaching the river they saw an enemy patrol of about 5 men who halted at some distance from the other side. The enemy patrol stopped 4 or 5 minutes and then retired. While waiting, our patrol could distinctly hear sounds of a hostile working party to their front, but could see nothing. The hostile patrol again moved to the same spot and retired as before after a short halt. Our patrol greatly appreciated the snow patrol suits. Other patrols examined the old German line, but found no signs of the enemy.

PART II INTELLIGENCE.

RIGHT SECTION. Hostile Artillery were active during the morning on TILLELOY C.T. in M.29.d. and later on in retaliation to our trench mortars in the same area. They were again active in the afternoon. A few hostile trench mortar shells fell near our lines about M.24.c.4.2., but no damage was caused. At 7.15 p.m. enemy observed moving about their parapet opposite M.24.2. trench. They were next seen at about M.24.d.1.3. A Very light was fired and five men were seen lying down wearing dark greatcoats and soft service caps. A Lewis gun opened fire on them and one man was seen to roll over and his cap fell off. A patrol was hastily organised, but by the time they were ready (a space of 3 minutes) the body had been removed. Tracks were followed to M.30.b.25.92., but no enemy discovered.
A hostile wiring party was heard at M.30.a.55.15. Lewis gun fired on them. At about 3 p.m. a light as though from a brazier was seen at M.30.c.6.9. Four men in all were seen at different times in the gap in the enemy front line about M.36.a.4.5.

LEFT SECTION. A few hostile shells were fired on to our C.Ts. during the afternoon. About 20 L.T.M. bombs were fired at ENFIELD Post. No damage caused, but the garrison had to vacate the post for half an hour. The L.T.M. was located firing from OSAKA Trench at M.19.d.25.65. Our Artillery were informed and fired with good effect causing the T.M. to cease firing.

/ The

(P.T.O)

The following is a detailed report of the enemy's movement seen from BERTHA Post yesterday:-
7.45 a.m. 3 men left dugout or M.G. emplacement at N.14.c.20.43. They were fired at. Another man who seemed too frightened to move was there until 12 noon. 8.30 a.m. Five men went N.W. from about N.19 central to N.19.a.50.25. where they disappeared. These men went at about 30 yards at a time and they crouched down and looked before proceeding again. They followed a black track with 5 elbow bends in it. 8.30 a.m. Nine men seen on the same track. These were probably the garrison of the German night post. ENFIELD POST saw a German suddenly appear and walk to a trench (probably the one at N.19.b.4.6.) where there were 4 or 5 more Germans. The party was fired at.

The usual movement was seen in MOSSY C.T. at N.20.b.30.65. and in AUBERS DEFENCES N.21.d.. Several parties were seen yesterday afternoon on the track at N.21.a.9.7. They were dispersed by our Artillery. Two small parties numbering 3 and 4 men were seen pushing trucks on the light railway and halting at the dump at N.21.b.30.15.

Hdqrs. 56th Divn.

18th January, 1917.

Lieutenant,
Intelligence, General Staff

56th DIVISIONAL TACTICAL PROGRESS REPORT No. 84.
from 8. 0 a.m. 18th January to 8. 0 a.m. 19th January 1917.

On receipt of current copy of Divisional Tactical Progress Report
in the trenches, previous copy to be destroyed.

PART I OPERATIONS.

RIGHT SECTION.- Our artillery and T.Ms. co-operated in a shoot on the enemy's trenches from M.30.a.85.15 to M.30.c.95.85. - results were very satisfactory. From 3.27 a.m. to 4. 0 a.m. our artillery and T.Ms. bombarded enemy's trenches in support of a raiding party which approached the enemy parapet at M.30.a.5.3. Enemy's trench was strongly manned, considerable rifle fire was opened when the party reached the wire. Full details have not yet arrived. A hostile machine gun which opened fire on this party from M.30. c.4.0 was silenced by our L.T.Ms.

One of our patrols entered the enemy lines at M.30.b.75.90. The wire is about 30 feet deep but so damaged that it presents no obstacle. The trench was very much battered and contained between 2 and 3 feet of water. The trolley lines in rear could not be found. A sniping post was discovered at point of entry constructed of timber and corrugated iron. The second line between M.30.b.5.9. and M.30.b.35.85 is not so well revetted as the front line. Another patrol located an enemy working party laying duck-boards about M.30.b.1.6. and enemy transport was heard in the direction of EVA Trench. The enemy wire at M.30.a.4.1. is low and damaged, but still forms a difficult obstacle. Another patrol reconnoitred the enemy Craters at M.36.c.1.9. A sentry was seen in the Southern most Crater wearing a snow suit. Three bombs were thrown into the Crater which drew rifle fire on to the patrol from M.36.c.11.90. The wire around the Craters is not good, and a small party can move with comparative ease.

LEFT SECTION.- Our artillery and H.T.Ms. co-operated in a bombardment on enemy posts, C.Ts. and workings along the RUE DELEVAL. Observation was difficult. A direct hit was observed on enemy post at N.14.c.2.4. duck-boards and sandbags were seen in the air. Later reports state that yesterday our artillery obtained 2 direct hits on the hostile T.M. firing from CLARA C.T. and 5 rounds of shrapnel burst over the team as they abandoned their gun. Our machine guns effectively barraged the enemy C.Ts. leading to our posts.

Our patrols kept in touch with the Posts all night and the old German line between the posts was reconnoitred. An old dugout was found 30 yards N. of IRMA POST. Twenty yards North of this there is an old bombing block. Beyond the block the trench was in fairly good condition for 200 yards. A C.T. was found at this point flooded, but otherwise in apparently good condition. Opposite the C.T. a stream runs towards our line with trees on the N.E.side. Footprints were seen in the snow on the British side here but no signs of the enemy were found. The trenches round WICK SALIENT are quite impassable. The tramway from N.14.a.7.2. was reconnoitred - it is very badly damaged. Working parties were heard on the enemy side of the river LAIES repairing the damage caused to the post by our shell fire.

PART II INTELLIGENCE.

RIGHT SECTION.- Hostile artillery was considerably more active than usual. They bombarded our C.Ts. and support line, several hits being obtained. Between 4.15 a.m. and 5. 0 a.m. the enemy replied vigorously to our bombardment. Enemy transport was heard on the AUBERS - BAS POMMEREAU Road and a train whistle from the direction of AUBERS. Three men were seen working at N.25.d.15.95. Two men and 1 Officer were seen at M.30.b.3.9 - they were sniped at - result not observed.

P.T.O. / LEFT SECTION.

LEFT SECTION. - Hostile artillery fired a few shells on to N.18.d.9.5. without doing any damage. Enemy Trench Mortar was again active from CLARA C.T. firing on to ENFIELD POST. The rounds all fell behind the post.

At 6.15 p.m. a hostile patrol, strength approximately 12 were seen advancing on to BERTHA POST. The artillery were immediately warned, and they opened fire very quickly indeed. Bombs were thrown at the enemy, rifle grenades/and indirect machine gun fire was opened and the patrol retired at once.

A small hostile working party was seen in the enemy post about N.19.a.4.3. - it was dispersed by machine gun fire. At 9.30 a.m. yesterday a small red balloon about 30" diameter passed over our line at N.8.c.35.00. towards the enemy. It fell in NO MAN'S LAND and was recovered last night.

Head Qrs. 56th Divn.
19th January, 1917.

Lieutenant,
Intelligence, General Staff.

56th DIVISIONAL TACTICAL PROGRESS REPORT No. 86.
from 8.0 a.m. 19th January to 8.0 a.m., 20th January, 1917.

On receipt of current copy of Divisional Tactical Progress Report in the trenches, previous copy to be destroyed.

PART I OPERATIONS.

RIGHT SECTION. Our Artillery confined themselves to registration and chastisement of enemy working parties yesterday. Our machine guns carried out intermittent firing on enemy C.Ts. and roads. Our patrols were out along the whole front, but could find no signs of the enemy. Coughing and a whistle were heard in the enemy second line at M.30.a.90.45. The road in M.35.d. running N.E. is now quite impassable, being 4' deep in water and 20' broad. Our snipers fired several shots at the enemy passing the gap at M.33.c.1.7. Result not observed.

LEFT SECTION. Our Artillery bombarded the following targets:- CLARA C.T., LOZENGE in N.19.a.9.5., house at N.25.b.8.9.(dump) and trench junctions. Our heavy trench mortars co-operated. Much damage was done, woodwork being seen in the air. Our machine guns sprayed the enemy C.Ts. during the night. One of our patrols reconnoitred IRMA C.T., moving along the South side. Enemy advanced post was located at N.14.a.85.20. The reflection of a light about 300x down IRMA C.T. was seen both by the patrol and by the garrison of IRMA Post. Other patrols could find no signs of the enemy.

PART II INTELLIGENCE

RIGHT SECTION. Hostile artillery were active. Our C.Ts. and reserve trenches all being shelled in the course of the day. No damage was caused, many of the shells being blind. Whilst the right battalion was wiring a hostile patrol was observed N. of MAUQUISSART Crater (M.30.c.10.35.) Fire was opened and they dispersed. Search for dead was without result. Usual movement was heard on the AUBERS - BAS POMMEREAU Road during the night. Several men were seen at WIRELESS House (T.2.b.2.7.) At 10.30 a.m. men wearing greatcoats were seen on the track behind the screened road at about N.25.d.5.7. Several holes have been knocked in this screen. About 2.p.m. a small party was seen moving along the support line at N.30.b.85.70. At 11.30.a.m. Germans were seen on the road at N.36.a.5.4. Smoke was seen at N.25.c.10.90. About 3.p.m. hostile aeroplane flew along our lines at a height of about 200 feet. It was fired upon by Lewis Guns and believed to have been hit. It disappeared towards PIETRE. Two semi-circular sheets of corrugated iron similar to our Elephant Iron Dugouts could be seen at N.31.d.50.03. Working parties were again seen in the new trench N.26.c.- N.32.a. Our Artillery dispersed these.

LEFT SECTION. Hostile Artillery fired a few shells on to FLAME POST, ENFIELD POST and Front Line in N.24.6. No serious damage was caused. Hostile M.G. firing from about N.14.c.10.25. was very troublesome on FLAME POST causing interruption of work. Another M.G. has been located at N.14.b.55.25. Hostile working parties were seen at N.20.c.30.98. and N.20.c.1.8. and N.26.b.95.00, near the house. Movement yesterday was considerably above normal. During the afternoon small parties were continually seen passing on the AUBERS - TROUELLES road between N.27.c.15.95 and N.23.d.9.8. The usual movement was seen on the tracks in N.15.c, N.21.a and around the Dump at N.21.b.50.15. Four men were seen walking N.E. along the RUE DELEVAL at N.14.d.70.45. Usual movement in MOSSY TRENCH at N.20.b.30.65. Much movement was observed near N.14.c.2.6. At 3.5.p.m. two men were seen to get out of HERTHA C.T. at N.14.c.42.15. and walk S.W. along side of trench for a few yards disappearing into trench again. The hostile aeroplane mentioned above fired a few rounds on N.13.d.

Hqrs.,56th Division.

20th January, 1916.

Lieutenant,
Intelligence, General Staff.

53th DIVISIONAL TACTICAL PROGRESS REPORT No. 87.
from 8.0 a.m. 21st January to 8.0 a.m. 21st January 1917.

On receipt of current copy of Divisional Tactical Progress Report
in the trenches, previous copy to be destroyed.

PART I OPERATIONS.
RIGHT SECTION. Our Artillery shelled various points in the enemy front line and support trenches including MIM DU PIETRE (M 30.A.9.9.). Our trench mortars fired on M.24.d.60.20. and M.24.d.51.15. Considerable damage was caused, parapet and woodwork being thrown into the air. One of our patrols examined the enemy wire from M.36.a.3.3. to M.36.a.55.55.It appears to be in good repair and forms a formidable obstacle. The ground in front of M.35.4 & 5. is very flooded. Another patrol entered the enemy trench at M.30.a.40.15. The parapet at the point of entry is about 7 or 8 feet in height. The wire is good, and about 12 feet in width. Behind the wire is a ditch about 6' wide and 4' deep. Behind the ditch there is more wire which affords small obstacle. The trenches are well revetted and contain about 2' of water. The party established one block at the point of entry and working northwards another at M.30.a.5.2. They then proceeded along the edge of the road to M.30.a.60.15. Here a trench was found in a very bad state of repair and unrevetted. This was followed and brought the party into the front line about 25ᵡ N. of the point of entry. The party moved S. to M.30.a.50.02. establishing a block and endeavoured to enter the short trench running E. but it was impassable. Two dugouts and what appeared to be a snipers post of concrete having a metal front with loophole was seen at M.30.a.45.10. There was evidence of recent use as several cartridges cases were seen. None of the enemy were seen or heard. Other patrols have nothing to report. One of our snipers claimed to have hit a German who was looking over the parapet at M.36.a.30.35.

LEFT SECTION. Our Artillery carried out a programme bombardment from 2 to 7 p.m. yesterday on the junction of C.Ts., RUE d'ENFER with RUE DELEVAL - houses N.15.a.1.5. and N.14.d.92.55. - works and M.G.Es. N.14.b.55.25. Several parties of the enemy seen in back areas were fired on and men were seen to be hit at N.20.b.85.40. Our machine guns were active during the afternoon and night firing on to enemy C.Ts. and RUE DELEVAL. One of our patrols examined the old German line from BERTHA Post to WICK Salient; about 80 yards S.W. of FLAME a concrete sniping post without a roof was found and another on WICK Salient. At WICK Salient there is only about 3" water in the trenches. Another patrol examined the ruins at N.19.a.00.65. and the enemy trench at N.19.a.3.5. Trench was found to be deserted and wet. The ruins form a round mound three to four feet high and 15 yards by 25 yards The ground around the ruins is flat provides little cover, and has a good field of fire in all directions. Everything was very quiet. No signs of the enemy were seen.

PART II INTELLIGENCE.
RIGHT SECTION.
Hostile Artillery was slight during the day, but during the night it was unusually active. Between 10 p.m. and 12 midnight, the LA BASSEE Road was shelled in M 54. A green light was sent up from this area and fire then searched towards the S. A red light was sent up and the fire then switched back again. Houses in the neighbourhood were searched by us without result. A large hostile working party was observed at 8.0 a.m. on the railway line in M.32.b. Dispersed by artillery. Coughing and noise of hammering heard at M.30.a.95.55. During the morning small parties were seen in the support line about M.30.d.85.70. Several men were seen on the track from about N.25.d.7.4. to N.25.d.90.75. Three men were seen on the road at M.36.a.6.7. One man was seen going along the C.T. at M.30.A.75.70. Four men were seen on the screened road N.25.d.10.90 At 3.55v p.m. five men passed along the C.T. at M.30.d. 65.70. and disappeared into EVA C.T. Several men were seen passing the gap at M.36.c.15.65. They were sniped at but results not observed. Smoke was seen near LA CLIQUETERIE Farm.

LEFT SECTION.
Between 6.45 and 7.15 p.m. the enemy shelled ENFIELD Post; our guns responded quickly. Hostile machine guns fired bursts during the night on to parapet of our old line and on to tracks out to the posts. The hostile trench mortar in CLARA C.T. again fired on to ENFIELD POST.

Our artillery replied with 28 rounds of 4.5" H.E. At 5.30 p.m. a small hostile party approached IRMA Post and threw a grenade which did no damage. Rifle and Lewis gun fire was opened on to them and they scattered and retired. New earth has been thrown up on the parapet at BERTHA C.T. at N.20.a.60.35. On three occasions yesterday a small party of three or four men was seen to get out of BERTHA C.T. at about N.20.a.9.7. and walk alongside the trench in a northerly direction for a few yards and then re-enter same. The movement in N.20.b. was above normal. Several small parties being observed on the track. Much movement was seen during the day on the AUBERS - BAS POMMEREAU Road, TRAMWAY Corner (N.26.a.60.26.) CLARA and BERTHA C.Ts. HAYSTACK O.P. (N.21.a.6.5.). A man was seen to get into the trench at N.14.d.28.90. with a large black box. The tramline at N.21.a.9.7. was in use during the day, men were also seen here carrying boxes. The drain from N.21.d.1.0. to N.21.c.85. appears to have been recently cleared out. Between 8.30 and 9.30 p.m. the enemy had a searchlight working behind his line covering the WICK Area. Smoke was seen at N.20.b.1.4. and N.20.b.30.55..

<u>German Power Cable.</u> Information having been received that a heavy armoured cable was protruding from the ground in the vicinity of IRMA Post, a corporal and 2 men from Brigade Signal Section were detailed to investigate. The line was located about 15 yards S.E. of the post, portions were stripped and tested with electric lamp for power and with telephone for signals. Being found "dead" a portion was sawn out. The cable consists of three conductors, each consisting of one centre heavy strand and 24 lighter strands laid round same of about 18 gauge copper. Each conductor insulated with Presspahn, Lead Pitched Presspahn, tarred hemp, two layers of steel ribbon and an outer covering of tarred hemp. This powerful cable must have been used for extremely strong currents

Hdqrs. 56th Divn.

21st January, 1917.

Lieutenant,

Intelligence, General Staff.

56th DIVISIONAL TACTICAL PROGRESS REPORT No. 88
from 8.0 a.m. 21st January to 8.0 a.m. 22nd January, 1917.

PART I OPERATIONS.

RIGHT SECTION. Our Artillery and trench mortars co-operated in a shoot on the enemy's support line, M.36.a; and strong point M.30.d.00.65. The enemy wire was much damaged by our trench mortars from M.30.c.55.85. to M.30.c.50.60. and M.30.c 38 12. to M 36.a.38.90. Many enemy working parties were dispersed during the day and our howitzers retaliated severely on "Minnie" No. 9. (M.30.c.30.07.) which fired a few rounds near MAUQUISSART Crater. Our patrols were out along the whole front but found no signs of the enemy. They ascertained that damage had been caused to our wire between M.35.b.85.25. and M.35.b.85.45. by enemy bombardment. This wiring is now well in hand.

LEFT SECTION. Under cover of a heavy bombardment of our posts, especially BERTHA, old NO MANS's LAND, front line trench, and C.Ts. commencing at about 5.45 p.m. the enemy occupied BERTHA Post. The garrison owing to the intensity of the fire moved to a flank and whilst so doing were attacked by hostile party. The Lewis gun and most of the garrison retired to our front line. A counter-attack was at once organised, but this was broken up by the two machine guns which the enemy had brought up and trained down the tracks leading to our old line and to FLAME Post. Later Our guns kept up a steady barrage behind BERTHA C.T. all night and our Stokes Mortars bombarded the post. A reconnaissance of the enemy position was made and at 5.30 a.m. under cover of a heavy Artillery and Stokes Mortar barrage we re-occupied the post. The hostile bombardment was very well directed and organised, evidently consequent upon the aerial reconnaissance carried out by a hostile aeroplane reported yesterday. One of our patrols reconnoitred the ground in front of IRMA Post to find out whether the enemy had any posts W. of the LAIES in that locality. The patrol followed IRMA C.T. on the southern side. Voices and sound of men walking on duck-board were heard at N.14.a.97.20. It is presumed that the enemy either have a post established there already or have parties working there with a view to doing so shortly, but no movement has been seen there in the daytime. The snow and thin ice made it very difficult for the patrol to move at all quietly. Usual visiting patrol kept in touch with posts. Our machine guns enfiladed BERTHA C.T. all night with indirect fire. During the day our artillery in co-operation with Stokes Mortars bombarded the enemy post in front of TRIVILET, and the works on DORA C.T. The shooting appeared to be very effective.

PART II INTELLIGENCE.

RIGHT SECTION. Hostile artillery were active in the morning on RUE TILLELOY about M.23.d. In the afternoon and evening portions of our front line were shelled, the fire becoming intense between 6 and 7 p.m., some damage being caused to our parapet. An enemy working party was heard between M.36.a.40.30. and M.36.a.40.40. Movement was seen on the roads between AUBERS and H.T.POMMEREAU. The enemy is attempting to screen the new trench in N.26.c. and N.32.a. with brushwood. The N.E. half is already thinly screened. Considerable movement was seen round the MIN du PIETRE, men being seen in the trench at M.30.d.85.70. on several occasions. At 10.15 a.m. three men in clean fatigue were seen about M.25.c.65.20. Working parties were dispersed during the day at LES MOTTES FME.
N.31.b.85.90.
N.32.b.85.30.(dump suspected)
N.31.a.80.85.
N.25.a.55.60.
N.25.d.90.10.
and smoke at M.30.d.87.85. The trench railway running through MIN du PIETRE was heard in use at stand to this morning.

LEFT SECTION. A heavy hostile trench mortar fired a few rounds on to our trenches in M.24.b. during the morning. It is thought to have fired either from the DISTILLERY or from CLARA C.T. This trench mortar also fired three heavy bombs on to our two southern posts at 12 noon, one was blind. Hostile machine guns were active, two guns were firing from the position directly in front of BARNET Post on to our working parties. A machine gun was also firing from the enemy post in front of TRIVILET. There was considerable activity in the last mentioned enemy post last night.

/During

During stand to rifles were fired from about N.19.a.30.10. to 30.20. At 9.15 p.m. orders were shouted and bombs were thrown. Two flares went up and a machine gun opened fire. This was repeated at 10.25 p.m. At 11.55 a.m. three men were observed walking N.W. along BERTHA C.T. and could be seen as far as N.14.c.3.3. Just before reaching this point three other men appeared and moved along the trench in a S.E. direction, the two parties passing at about N.20.a.60.95. All men wore overcoats, soft caps, and carried rifles, but no equipment could be distinguished. At 3.45 p.m. one man was seen at N.14.c.30.38. moving S.E. The trench appears to be in a bad state as the above men clambered along the revetting in several places offering good targets for snipers in our advanced post. At 2.0 p.m. our artillery bombarded the enemy line where RUE DELEVAL crosses MOSSY Trench (N.20.b.1.9.) Immediately after arrival of first round 12 men were seen to run along track at N.20.b.95.25. towards 14 TREE CLUMP in a disorderly manner. During the day a few men were seen walking on RUE DELEVAL, also working on AUBERS DEFENCES at N.21.d.8.1. Smoke was seen N.20.b.1.3. dugout, N.21.d.75.15. AUBERS DEFENCES. During the hostile bombardment at about 6.0 p.m. last night, bearings taken from M.12.a.3.9. on flashes.

True bearing $159°30'$ Believed to be No.136 T.14.b. 85.50.

True bearing $141°30'$ Believed to be No.135 N.33.b. 1.2.

F.C.Heald

Hdqrs. 56th Divn.   Lieutenant,

22nd January, 1917.   Intelligence, General Staff.

On receipt of current copy of Divisional Tactical Progress Report in the trenches, previous copy to be destroyed.

56th DIVISIONAL TACTICAL PROGRESS REPORT No. 89.
from 8.0 a.m. 22nd January to 8.0 a.m. 23rd January, 1917.

On receipt of current copy of Divisional Tactical Progress Report in the trenches, previous copy to be destroyed.

PART I OPERATIONS.

RIGHT SECTION. Our artillery registered yesterday the enemy defences round HAUT POMMEREAU and dispersed working parties at M.30.d.99.82. and N.35.c.85.60. Our trench mortars fired on M.30.a.60.23. and machine gun emplacement at M.30.c.55.93., considerable damage being caused. One of our patrols inspected the enemy wire from M.35.d.93.41. to the left for 50 yards. The enemy seemed very suspicious and continually sent up Very lights. The crater at M.36.c.90.10. is unoccupied, but the wire in front forms a good obstacle. This patrol was fired on from about M.36.c.18.68. Other patrols were out but reported everything quiet and no signs of the enemy.

LEFT SECTION. Our artillery fired chiefly on working parties and suspected crossings of the River LAIES. During the night the enemy seems to have made an organised attempt to capture our posts and thus re-occupy his front line. About 6.30 p.m. an enemy patrol approached IRMA Post from the N. This was at once detected by our patrol which was constantly covering the ground in front of the post, fire was opened and the enemy retired. Our patrol did not find any casualties. At 8.0 p.m. under rifle grenades and trench mortar fire a party of the enemy attempted to rush BERTHA Post, but was repulsed by rifle and Lewis gun fire assisted by our artillery which opened very rapidly. A wiring party went out as soon as it was quiet but fire was opened on to them and the w. much interfered with. About 11 p.m. a hostile artillery barrage was put up on the post and enemy parties advanced from left flank and front and commenced bombing. The garrison replied with bombs and held on for some time, but were eventually forced to evacuate the post. The post was again re-occupied by us at 4.30 a.m.

At 7.45 p.m. a party of 20 - 30 Germans came into contact with our wiring party to the right of ENFIELD Post. The wiring party opened fire and reinforced BARNET and ENFIELD Posts. The enemy lay down under our Lewis gun and rifle fire. Support platoons were extended in NO MANS LAND on the outer flanks of posts. The enemy managed to get away in the darkness. Our trench mortars co-operated energetically in defence of the posts whilst our machine guns enfiladed the C.Ts. leading to these posts.

PART II INTELLIGENCE.

RIGHT SECTION. Hostile artillery were active during the day firing chiefly on our reserve line and C.Ts. No great damage was caused; a large percentage being blind. A few hostile M.T.M. bombs fell near MAUQUISSART Crater M.30.c.1.4. At 9.30 a.m. much transport was heard behind the enemy lines in rear of BOIS du BIEZ. The trench railway running through MIN du PIETRE was also in use during the night. Enemy working parties were seen at the following points and were dispersed: 9.30 a.m. in trench at M.36.c.28.50., 11.0 a.m. in trench from M.36.c.85.15. to S.3.a.68.70., men at house on road M.36.b.05.72., GRETCHEN C.T. at M.36.b.70.50.

At M.36.a.60.95. large volumes of smoke were seen at 8.0 a.m. Several men were observed in the ruins of MIN du PIETRE. At 9.45 a.m. 2 men were seen in a field walking in a N.W. direction, they disappeared into the trench at M.36.a.55.20. Two men were observed at M.30.b.20.50. Smoke was seen at M.36.a.41.54.
M.36.a.50.10.
M.36.a.18.92.
LA CLIQUETERIE FME (T.3.a.)

LEFT SECTION. Hostile artillery and trench mortars were active during the day shelling our posts, developing into a bombardment at 6 p.m. and again at 11.0 p.m. on BERTHA Trench. The German party which occupied BERTHA Trench brought up a machine gun which they used energetically.

/Much

- 2 -

Much transport was heard during the night. Between 7 p.m. and 12 midnight, whistles and trains were heard. Much movement was seen in BERTHA C.T. yesterday. At 10.45 a.m. a man wearing equipment and carrying a rifle clambered over the E. parapet of trench at N.14.c.33. and proceeded cautiously in a S.E. direction under cover of the trench reentering the same at N.20.a.85.80. This was repeated an hour later. At 11.50 a.m. two men left the trench at N.20.a.9.7. moving in a southerly direction. At 1 p.m. a man was seen in the trench at N.15.d.95.25. going towards BERTHA, 10 minutes later three more men were seen at the same place. At 2.20 p.m. a man was seen to fire one round with his rifle from the trench at N.20.a.5.3. A few mintes minutes later he was seen to join a small party of 4 or 5 men wearing cloth caps and rifles slung at N.20.a.85.20. This party then proceeded to work in the trench very vigorously. Our artillery immediately opened and all movement ceased. At 2.25 p.m. eight men crawled from N.14.d.20.20. to BERTHA C.T. and commenced digging. Our Hows. obtained a direct hit, one man ran away across the open at 4 p.m. A man in a steel helmet was seen in the damaged C.T. at about N.15.c.10.90. Several small parties of men were seen on track at N.20.b.95.25. and were dealt with by our artillery. Working parties were also seen on AUBERS Defences at N.20.b.95.25. and dispersed by our Artillery. Movement was observed round the house at N.20.d.45.95. At 6.55 p.m. a searchlight again swept our parapet. Flares were sent up from N.19.c.15.80. and N.19.a.3.1. Smoke was seen at N.20.b.20.45.

T.L.C. Heald

Hdqrs. 56th Divn.

23rd January, 1917.

Lieutenant,

Intelligence, General Staff.

56th DIVISIONAL TACTICAL PROGRESS REPORT No. 90.
from 8.0 a.m. 23rd January to 8.0 a.m. 24th January, 1917.

On receipt of current copy of Divisional Tactical Report in the trenches, previous copy to be destroyed.

PART I OPERATIONS

RIGHT SECTION. Our artillery co-operated with our trench mortars in a bombardment of the enemy trenches at M.30.a.65.15. to M.30.d.00.75, GRETCHEN C.T. and M.36.a.40.90. Our heavy trench mortars fired chiefly on the enemy front line in M.36.a.. All the shooting was very satisfactory. Hostile retaliation was heavy. In addition, our artillery obtained five direct hits on an O.P. known to be occupied at M.31.b.85.62. One of our patrols examined the enemy's wire around M.30.c.55.55. and reported it to be badly damaged. The wire in front of M.36.c.15.70. was also reported to be in a poor condition. A small reconnoitring patrol entered the enemy trench at M.30.a.85.50.; it was found to be badly damaged and the wire in front presented no obstacle. Very lights were being sent up from the direction of the house at M.30.c.97.80. The patrol listended for a while at M.30.a.90.20., but could hear nothing nor were any enemy seen

LEFT SECTION. Our artillery carried out counter offensive action to enemy shelling of BERTHA and ENFIELD Posts. A slow barrage was put up in front of our posts during relief. Our 6" Hows. shelled the houses in LE PIETRE, and BERTHA C.T., whilst our medium trench mortars bombarded M.19.a.3.1. Our machine guns fired intermittently all day and night down CLARA, BERTHA and DORA C.Ts. A patrol relieved every three hours, patrolled continuously round flanks and in front of IRMA Post. The trench in which the enemy party was located and fired on last night was examined, and a German rifle was found there. It was quite clean and evidently had not been there more than a day or two. No signs of the enemy were heard or seen. Other patrols had nothing to report. Our working parties took advantage of the enemy's inactivity and much work and wiring were carried out on our posts.

PART II INTELLIGENCE.

RIGHT SECTION. Hostile artillery and trench mortars were very active during the afternoon chiefly on the front line at M.29.1. and M.29.2. Our C.Ts. also received attention, a few direct hits being obtained. An M.T.M. bomb dropped in a dump of our trench mortar ammunition causing a great explosion. A large crater was formed and the railway was destroyed at M.34.b.75.38. Three hostile patrols were seen and fired on: they dispersed very rapidly towards their own trench. Much railway transport was heard between 8 and 9 a.m. An enemy working party seen at M.36.b.05.72. and M.36.c.78.50. was dispersed by our fire. At 11.30 a.m. hostile aeroplane over our lines was fired at with Lewis guns and rifles. Shelling shortly afterwards seemed to be result of the observation. 11.50 a.m. two men seen amongst ruins MIN du PIETRE. 2.0 p.m. Two men seen M.36.a.35.30. 2.15 p.m. Two men seen in FRIEDA Trench M.31.a.65.55. 2 men crossed open ground towards FRIEDA Trench, N.31.a.85.55. 3.0 p.m. 2 cyclists observed riding from BAS POMMEREAU towards junction at N.25.c.65.15., they turned left and disappeared towards PIETRE. 3.15 p.m. 3 men carrying shovels moved along Support trench at M.30.d.85.70. Green Very lights were fired by enemy during the night.

LEFT SECTION. Hostile artillery were active shelling our front and support lines. Little material damage was done, only one bay being blown in. Hostile trench mortars co-operated with their artillery in shelling our posts at night. A bearing taken on one of the flashes crosses CLARA Trench at about N.19.d.40.45. Sounds of hammering were heard between 8 and 8.30 a.m. coming from the old enemy line between TRIVELET and DORA C.T.. Sounds of breaking ice
/ were

were heard from the enemy post near the DISTILLERY M.19.c.6.0.
Machine gun is suspected at M.19.a.3.2. at 11.30 a.m. three men
walked from the trench at N.14.d.2.1. and disappeared behind the
barricade. New work can be seen on BERTHA C.T. at N.14.c.35.20.
At 2.0 p.m. a man looked over the barricade on the road at
M.20.d.8.5. Smoke was seen at N.19.d.25.60. CLARA C.T.;
N.20.b.5.0. house Little movement was again seen on the track
at N.20.b.95.25. and in N.21.a.

Hdqrs. 56th Divn.

24th January, 1917.

T.A.Heald

Lieutenant,
Intelligence, General Staff.

56th DIVISIONAL TACTICAL PROGRESS REPORT No. 91.
from 8. 0 a.m. 24th January to 8. 0 a.m. 25th January 1917.

On receipt of current copy of Divisional Tactical Progress
Report in the trenches, previous copy to be destroyed

PART 1 OPERATIONS.

RIGHT SECTION. - Our T.Ms. all calibres had a combined shoot on pro-arranged targets in the enemy trenches.
Our artillery gave supporting fire on points just in rear. One of our patrols examined the enemy wire at M.36.a.35.50. They reported that the wire had been sufficiently destroyed to allow a party to get through. A sentry opened fire on the patrol from about M.36.a.35.47 and a machine gun from the direction of the Crater at M.36.a.25.25. Another patrol approached the enemy parapet at about M.30.b.35.95. and left 4 men there. They then proceeded to the Crater at M.24.d.26.13. - this appears to be disused, and there is no communication between it and the German front line. The patrol then proceeded to the German front line trench which they patrolled from M.24.d.42.02. to M.24.d. 45.10. where the C.T. was located with difficulty. The patrol endeavoured to get up the C.T. but it was impassable so they proceeded over the top with the intention of locating the railway. No signs of this could be found, but there were considerable number of planks and wire lying about. The patrol returned along the parapet of the supervision trench to the C.T. at M.24.d.55.00. where they discovered a track which appears to be used by hostile patrols. (this track is clearly visible on air photo No. 10 A 691) The patrol advanced up this path for about 100 yards to a stream running at right angles to the C.T. There are fire steps and one narrow plank in this C.T. Sounds of the enemy shouting were heard about 200 yards to the left. Owing to the path being so conspicuous the patrol withdrew, without casualties.
One of our snipers claims a hit at M.36.c.30.60.

LEFT SECTION. - Our artillery searched DORA C.T. from 11 to 11.45 a.m. A Howitzer Battery fired on the Distillery Chimney. Our H.T.Ms. fired on to N.19.c.25.10. with good results. At 7. 0 p.m. the enemy began an intense bombardment of BERTHA POST and our front line behind. This gradually became less intense ceasing about 9. 0 p.m. The garrison and working parties suffered severely from this fire but no infantry action resulted.
At 7.50 p.m. a party of 6 Germans was seen to approach BARNET POST from the left - this was dispersed by our Lewis Gun.
At 8.30 p.m. Very Lights were sent up from the old German line 100 yards to the left of BARNET POST. These landed behind our Posts and on the tracks. The Germans made use of light for sniping.
At 8.57 p.m. 30 Germans advanced along their old line to attack BARNET. They were able to obtain cover in their old trench owing to the hard ice. They then extended 50 yards to the left and attacked in a wave. They were held up with bombs and L.G. fire until a supporting platoon which had been held ready in our front line reinforced the Post, when after a fight lasting 10 minutes the enemy were driven off. Our Stokes Mortars put a barrage in front of the Posts immediately the alarm was given. It is believed that casualties were inflicted on the enemy, but a patrol which was sent out was unable to find any owing to wire and other obstacles. Whilst the attack was in progress a further party tried to get in between the two posts but were driven off by our sentry group stationed there. Our artillery covered the crossings over the river LAIES with shrapnel to catch the retreating enemy. At 7. 0 p.m. a hostile patrol which attempted to reach IRMA POST was dispersed by rifle fire and Lewis Guns. Our M.Gs. kept up their usual night firing down all enemy communication trenches.

/PART II INTELLIGENCE

2.

PART II INTELLIGENCE.

RIGHT SECTION.- Hostile artillery were very active yesterday, our C.Ts and support lines being shelled. Hostile T.Ms. fired on to M.29.2. and to our extreme right. The position of MINNIE. No. 2 M.36.c.20.10. is confirmed. Enemy transport was heard between 8.30 and 9.30 p.m. apparently on RUE D'ENFER.
Enemy working parties were seen and dispersed at M.36.a. 40.35. M.36.c.21.50. and N.33.a.00.60.
Occasionally men were observed in support line at M.30.d. 85.70. Two men climbed out of the trench at N.31.a.85.60. and made off across country.
At 2.45 p.m. train whistle was heard from the direction of MARQUILLES. Two Germans seen wearing greatcoats and spiked helmets at N.25.c.30.05. are thought to be officers.
A party wearing white bands round their hats were seen at M.26.c.32.66.
Smoke was seen at M.36.a.40.70.
and N.31.a.20.35
Gas was detected at 5.50 p.m. probably from a gas shell from the left.

LEFT SECTION. - Hostile artillery and T.Ms. were very active.
Our Posts front line, tracks, C.Ts. and the RUE TILLELOY were all shelled systematically. It was reported that the enemy were using lachrymatory T.M. Bombs. The garrison of ENFIELD POST was forced to wear respirators. Much transport was heard in AUBERS during the night. An L.T.M. was located at N.19.d.27.85. Much movement was seen in DORA C.T. BERTHA C.T. and on RUE DELEVAL five large mounds can be seen in the AUBERS Defences from N.27.a.9.9. to 5.5. Movement is seen near them continuously. Doors and stops can be distinguished in two of them.
A party of five men, and a little later another party of three men, were seen walking S.E. along light railway at N.21. a.88.70.
At 3.20 p.m. two loaded trucks were being pushed S.E. by five men, along light railway at N.21.d.7.8. Our artillery were informed of the above targets.
At 3.15 p.m. 2 men were seen to leave house at N.27.a.65.20 and walk N.E. along the AUBERS-FROMELLES ROAD.
During the afternoon a hostile bty. (4.2") was located by sound and time bearings   and also bearings on the flash as No. 149 - N.34.a.50.65.

Head Qrs. 56th Divn.
25th January, 1917.

Lieutenant,
Intelligence, General Staff.

56th DIVISIONAL TACTICAL PROGRESS REPORT No. 92.
from 8.0 a.m. 25th January to 8.0 a.m. 26th January, 1917.

On receipt of current copy of Divisional Tactical Progress Report in the trenches, previous copy to be destroyed.

PART I OPERATIONS.

RIGHT SECTION. Our artillery fired on the enemy trenches at the following points:- M.30.c.60.60., M.30.c.15.55., M.36.a.30.10. We retaliated on the O.P. at N.25.a.04.14. for the enemy shelling of CHAPIGNY. Our heavy trench mortars fired on the enemy front line about M.36.a.30.30. with very effective results whilst our M.T.Ms. engaged various targets in M.30.a. Results, very satisfactory. At 11 p.m. one of our patrols approached the enemy line at about M.36.a.38.60. with the intention of entering the trench. A party of about 25 Germans were repairing the wire which was cut yesterday, so this patrol withdrew. This patrol went out again at 12.15 a.m. They found that the wire had been sufficiently repaired to prevent them rushing the post and, whilst endeavouring to find a way through they were fired on, three men being hit. The patrol withdrew to our lines bringing with them the casualties. Other patrols were out but have nothing to report. One of our snipers claims a victim at M.24.d.60.30.

LEFT SECTION. Our heavy trench mortars and medium trench mortars carried out a short bombardment of the strong point in enemy trench running from N.19.c.20.80. to 35.65. Our Artillery provided the covering fire. Results were very satisfactory. Our guns also shelled LE PIETRE. Our machine guns fired on to the tracks which have been located by aeroplane photograph as used by the enemy. Our patrols constantly reconnoitred the ground in front of and between our posts, but could find no signs of the enemy.

PART II INTELLIGENCE.

RIGHT SECTION. Hostile artillery was fairly active during the afternoon on various points in our defences, but no damage was caused. Hostile trench mortars fired a few rounds towards N.35.b.70.05. Two hostile machine guns were located to be firing at our aeroplanes from M.36.c.35.70. and M.36.a.47.55. Heavy transport was heard in rear of enemy' lines at 6 p.m., 11 p.m., and 11.30 p.m. Movement seemed to be from N. to S. Sounds of talking were heard opposite M.29.3a. between 8 and 9 p.m. At 8.30 a.m. an engine whistle was heard from behind AUBERS. At 11.20 a.m. a man was seen in the fields near the cross roads at N.25.c.65.25. Also much movement was again observed in the ruins of the MIN du PIETRE. Three men were seen behind the enemy front line at M.36.c.15.30. At 1.15 p.m. men were observed walking along C.T. at M.30.d.85.70. at intervals. Movement is seen here every day. Smoke was seen ascending from N.25.b.10.90. Movement was also seen at M.36.a.52.70., M.36.c.30.65. and 12.68.

LEFT SECTION. Hostile artillery were much quieter than usual, but BERTHA and IRMA Posts were shelled at intervals during the night. A few light trench mortar shells fell on BARNET and ENFIELD, probably fired from CLARA C.T. At 8.15 p.m. a hostile party of about 15 strong was seen approaching IRMA Trench Post, they were dispersed by our Lewis gun and rifle fire. At 11.45 p.m., a party of six men were seen on the enemy parapet at N.19.a.3.6. Lewis approaching ENFIELD POST. Lewis gun fire was directed on them and they dispersed. Flares were fired by the Germans from their old front line about N.8.d.3.1. and also from their post about N.19.a.3.1. Four loopholes can be seen at N.19.a.3.6. It is thought that a machine gun fired from there yesterday. Usual movement was seen on the track at N.20.b.05.35. During the day a few men were seen walking in a S.W. direction on the track at N.15.c.6.2. including two men wearing steel helmets, one of them looked like and officer carrying a stick. Two men hurriedly left the wood at N.15.c.85.10. carrying duxies and ran across the open to about N.21.a.40.75. where they disappeared. About an hour later they returned with the dixies

P.T.O.

apparently full, across the same route to the wood. Five men wearing equipment and carrying rifles walked along the RUE DELEVAL at N.14.d.75.45. in a S.W. direction. Much movement was seen on the AUBERS Defences in N.37.a. and N.21.d. At 5 p.m. large parties were seen on the track about N.20.a.95.80. Smoke was seen at N.19.d.7.7., N.20.a.9.9. N.20.a.9.6½. and N.20.a.8.5.

T.F.C.Heald

Hdqrs. 56th Divn.
26th January, 1917.

Lieutenant,
Intelligence, General Staff.

56th DIVISIONAL TACTICAL PROGRESS REPORT No. 93
from 8.0 a.m. 26th January to 8.0 a.m. 27th January 1917.

On receipt of current copy of Divisional Tactical Progress Report
in the trenches, previous copy to be destroyed.

PART I OPERATIONS.

RIGHT SECTION.- Our artillery carried out a registration of the enemy trenches about M.30.c.58.84. Our M.Gs. carried out their usual programme of night firing on the cross roads in PIETRE and N.25.c. 85.15. One of our patrols entered the German front line trenches at M.34.d.5.1. there were no signs of occupation.

A hostile patrol of 8 men were seen close to the second line but these quickly disappeared. Other patrols were out along the whole front but no signs of the enemy were seen or heard.

The relief of 168th Brigade by 167th Brigade was completed by 10.30 p.m. without incident.

LEFT SECTION.- Our artillery except for registration were quiet yesterday. Our T.Ms. breached the enemy parapet at N.19.c.18.92. Our M.Gs. liberally sprayed the tracks used by the Germans to reach their front positions. One of our patrols reconnoitred the river Laies in front of IRMA POST - no crossings were discovered that would be practicable in wet weather. It is thought, however, that the route used by the enemy to approach this post is alongside the tramway from N.14.b.80.65. Aeroplane photograph No. 10 A 700 shows tracks along this route. A small listening post was established at about N.14.b.05.85. who heard sounds of talking and blowing of noses at approximately N.14.a.95.60. It is evident that the Germans either establish posts or constantly patrol the SUGAR LOAF by night as aeroplane photographs show many tracks leading to this area. Another patrol established a post at N. 13.d.65.57. during the night, but no sign of the enemy was seen or heard. Other patrols were out in front of the post, but have nothing to report.

PART II INTELLIGENCE.

RIGHT SECTION.- Hostile artillery and T.Ms. were comparatively inactive yesterday. The enemy seems to be constructing a breastwork along the RUE DELEVAL about N.25.d.9.6. and N.25.b.2.1. He has also been showing much activity lately in the MIN DU PIETRE. Working parties being frequently seen here and movement reported every day. It seems to be one of the strong posts in his line of defences which run about 700 yards in rear of his front line. Recent aeroplane photograph show that the new trench joining the MIN DU PIETRE to DORA C.T. has been completed, and there are two thick bands of wire in front of it. This band of wire runs in a N.E. direction to LE PIETRE and from thence to FME DELEVAL, and is probably defended by machine guns firing from strong points on the main C.Ts. i.e. MIN DU PIETRE, LES MOTTES FME, Ruins at N.25.b.80.90. strong point at M.20.d.05.85. and ruins at N.14. d.90.55.

LEFT SECTION.- Hostile artillery was fairly active during the day, the fire being distributed over a wide area. IRMA POST, however, received a few shells at regular intervals throughout the night.

A hostile L.T.M. fired on to IRMA POST during the night. At 5.55 p.m. a small party of the enemy were seen approaching ENFIELD Post from the South. Our supports doubled out and enemy were dispersed by rifle and Lewis Gun fire. This party was moving along their old front line from the direction of their post near TRIVELET. At 10.30 p.m. about 15 - 20 Germans were seen on the left flank of IRMA POST; they were dispersed with rifle grenades L.G. fire and bombs. Flares were fired by the enemy from about N.14.a.95.60. and from further back. Trains were heard behind AUBERS at 9.15 p.m. At about N.14.b.7.2. in front of the

/screens

2.

screens on RUE DELEVAL. A little fresh timber is visible. Movement was seen on the tracks in N.20.b. and N.15.c.   At 7.30 a.m. a man was seen in the trench at N.14.c.6.8. and later a man behind the screen at N.13.d.9.2.

    Smoke was seen at M.20.d.50.08 house
                        M.20.d.90.10   "
                        M.20.b.15.45 dugout.
                        N.27.b.   LECLERCQ FME.

Head Qrs. 56th Divn.
27th January, 1917.

                                      Lieutenant,
                        Intelligence, General Staff.

56th DIVISIONAL TACTICAL PROGRESS REPORT No. 04.
from 8.0 a.m. 27th to 8.0 a.m. 28th January, 1917.

On receipt of current copy of Divisional Tactical Progress Report
in the trenches, previous copy to be destroyed.

PART I OPERATIONS.

LEFT SECTION. Our artillery carried out an offensive shoot during the
morning on the trench just N. of IRMA. ELEPHANT N.14.b.5.3. (tracks
to which can be seen on air photograph) IRMA C.T. and LE PIETRE.
A further bombardment became necessary during the evening in reply to
a hostile burst of intense fire on IRMA Post. Results very satisfactory.
Our machine guns enfiladed enemys C.Ts. a continuous fire being maintained
at the end of and following hostile bombardment of IRMA Post. At 7 p.m.
hostile artillery and trench mortars bombarded IRMA Post causing great
damage. About 7.50 p.m. we evacuated the post. Patrols then reconnoitred
the ground in the vicinity and found that a strong body of the enemy had
moved into IRMA Post. Our Stokes mortars and artillery then bombarded
the post. During the early morning our patrols attempted to approach the
post from the flanks but found large covering parties on either side.
About 5.5 a.m. after a short bombardment a strong
patrol re-occupied the post without opposition. It was very much damaged
by hostile shell fire so a new post was established 100 yards to the right
before dawn. One of our patrols reconnoitred the ground in front of
BARNET and ENFIELD. The patrol followed the German C.T. at M.13.c.6.0.
for some 150 yards striking the German second line which they searched
for another 150 yards. This was much damaged, with loose wire in front,
no signs of the enemy were seen or heard. Another patrol reported that
the old German front line is patrolled by the enemy from the SUGAR LOAF
to N.14.b.2.0. Voices were heard and several Very lights fired from this
trench during the night. Other patrols reconnoitred the ground all round
IRMA Post whilst the Germans were in occupation. After reconnoitring
the enemy trenches just N. of WICK Salient, a post was established at
approximately N.13.d.4.6. at 5.0 a.m. this morning.

RIGHT SECTION. Our artillery carried out registration on various points
in the enemy lines. and dispersed parties of the enemy seen at MOULIN du PIETRE,
N.25.a.05.14., N.32.a.0.00., N.26.b.82.30. and LES MOTTES FME. Our
light trench mortars carried out a small bombardment of the enemy
trenches at M.30.a.95.35. An enemy working party had been seen and
heard at this point, his work was greatly damaged, much material being
thrown in the air. Our machine guns fired on to the enemy communications
during the night. Our patrols reconnoitred ground opposite the right
subsection, but/enemy were seen. Reports from the left are not yet to
hand.

PART II INTELLIGENCE.

LEFT SECTION. Hostile artillery were fairly active during the day, our
O.Ts. and posts being shelled slightly. At 7.0 p.m. IRMA Post was
very heavily bombarded for five minutes with 77 mm. and 4.2" shells
from a concentration of guns. Shooting was very accurate. Hostile
trench mortars co-operated in this shoot. During the afternoon two
columns of transport were seen on the AUBERS - BAS POMMEREAU Road
at about N.26.c.65.10. apparently light limbers. The bend in the road
at this point has apparently been cleared, snow being heaped up either
side and it is thought that this road is much used at night. Usual
movement was seen around AUBERS Defences in M.21.d. and M.27.a.
At 3 p.m. two men appeared on the track at N.21.a.9.9. carrying what
were apparently machine gun ammunition boxes; the boxes were evidently
full and were placed on a truck on the tramway and pushed along to a
point about N.22.c.35.40. where they disappeared. New woodwork can be
seen in BERTHA C.T. from N.14.c.35.35. to N.14.c.6.0. During the
afternoon small parties in single file were seen to leave DORA C.T.
at N.25.d.65.95.

/ RIGHT SECTION.

RIGHT SECTION. Hostile artillery and trench mortars were inactive. Much work was seen to be taking place on the new trench N.26.c. to N.32.a. They were fired on by our artillery. At 4 p.m. a light locomotive apparently motor driven and drawing three trucks was seen moving in a S.W. direction, bearings taken on it cut railway line in N.32.c. but observer reports that it seemed farther back and nearer WIRELESS HOUSE T.2.b.2.7., but no such railway appears on the map. About 10 men were seen in the trucks and when the locomotive came to a standstill the men quickly unloaded the trucks. this was repeated 15 minutes later. The men were plainly visible. A man was seen to dump a small black box or case at N.31.b.30.40. and then lay out a wire in an E. direction -
2.45 p.m. movement seen in FRIEDA Trench M.30.d.6.4. in S. direction.
2.30 p.m. cyclists on road N.31.b.80.05. ? moving in an N.E. direction and wearing satchels.

Hdqrs. 56th Divn.

26th January, 1917.

T.C.Heald

Lieutenant,

Intelligence, General Staff.

56th DIVISIONAL TACTICAL PROGRESS REPORT No. 95.
from 8.0 a.m. 28th January to 8.0 a.m. 29th January, 1917.

On receipt of current copy of Divisional Tactical Progress Report in the trenches, previous copy to be destroyed.

PART I OPERATIONS.

RIGHT SECTION.- Our artillery carried out registration on point M.32.c.40.90. They also dispersed working parties seen at M.32.b.20.35. and parties on the road at N.32.c.25.85 N.26.c. 70.30. and MIN DU PIETRE. Our Stokes Mortars bombarded the sniper's post at M.30.a.45.10. and later the enemy trench at M.36.a.41.50 where smoke had been seen. The shooting was very effective in both cases and enemy retaliation feeble. Our M.Gs fired on the enemy communications and MIN DU PIETRE during the night.

One of our patrols examined the enemy sap opposite DUCK'S BILL (M.35.d.98.98.) from which it was thought there was a good deal of sniping. This sap, however, was found to be unoccupied but they discovered an enemy post 30 yards to the left which was occupied, a man being seen to strike a match - position about M.36.a.35.30. This post will be dealt with.

Other patrols entered the enemy line at the following points (1) M.30.a.40.15. The trench at this point is blown in and shows no signs of recent occupation. A working party was heard well to the North. (2) M.30.a.5.0., trench in bad condition. They found a hose pipe running back to the enemy support line. (3) M.30.c.55.90. - trench badly damaged. Sounds of coughing etc. were heard at about M.30.c.30.80. A further patrol which entered the enemy trench at M.30.a.45.15 penetrated about 200 yards to the road. There was no sign of the enemy.

Another patrol examined the Craters at M.30.a.60.60. They saw movement in enemy front line at M.30.a.80.60. thought to be a sentry group. The Craters were unoccupied. Movement was also heard in M.30.b.1.6.,

Other patrols reconnoitred the Crater at M.24.d.23.15, near which enemy patrols had been seen the previous night. An enemy working party of about 15 was located at M.30.b.45.95. and L.Gs. were trained on the spot. A patrol went out immediately after but could find no signs of the enemy. A fighting patrol entered the enemy lines at M.24.d.50.15. and M.30.b.22.80. but could find no signs of the enemy. At both places the wire was fairly thick although a good deal cut.

LEFT SECTION.- Our 6" Hows. carried out a bombardment of a section of BERTHA TRENCH at N.20.a.75.90. with the view of destroying it. The shooting was very accurate and it is hoped that this will have the effect of bringing large working parties on to the scene for our bombardment commencing 8.30 p.m. tonight. Our T.Ms. fired on to the enemy post in N.19.a.30.12. and our old IRMA POST, whilst our M.Gs. sprayed C.Ts., RUE DELEVAL and LE PIETRE at intervals.

One of our patrols attempting to approach IRMA POST at 5.30 p.m. was fired upon by a machine gun, so we bombarded the point with Stokes Mortars and rifle grenades, which had the effect of driving the enemy out. Our patrol then entered and brought back the body of one of our men who had been killed the previous evening. Other patrols reconnoitred the German line at various points finding no signs of the enemy except in HAMPSTEAD POST N.19.a.3.1.

The permanent posts in the German front line were withdrawn and all stores cleared before "Stand to" this morning. Parties were out cutting the wire anchorages holding back the revetments of the German trenches, good progress was made. In places the wire was too thick for our cutters to grip.

/INTELLIGENCE

PART II INTELLIGENCE.

RIGHT SECTION.- Hostile artillery fired a few shrapnel and H.E. Shell in reply to our L.T.M. shoot, but no damage was caused. Some 4.2's also fell along the RUE TILLELOY. Enemy transport was heard in the direction of MIN DU PIETRE about 12.30 a.m. New work can be seen at MIN DU PIETRE. Much movement was again seen around the new trench in N.26.c. to N.32.a. Most of the men were observed to be carrying rifles. Three men were seen mending telephone wires at N.26.b.85.30. The shrine in N.32.c. recently destroyed by our artillery and the debris of the building has been cleared away by the enemy. Movement was also seen at M.36.a.30.70. M.36.a.30.35. M.30.c.55.10. M.36.b.05.70. and in GRETCHEN C.T. Smoke was seen M.36.a.30.20 LES MOTTE FARM and DORA C.T. (N.25.a.35.98.)

LEFT SECTION.- Hostile artillery was much less active than usual. Slight shelling of IRMA POST.

At 7.30 p.m. our patrol at M.13.d.60.55 observed a party of 5 Germans on the far side of the River LAIES. They dispersed them with Lewis Gun.

At 5.30 p.m. our patrol at N.14.a.70.25. where we had established a small post, observed a party of Germans moving in extended order towards them. When nearing the parapet they closed to a flank in order to encircle the right flank of the post. Lewis Gun fire was opened and they retired hurriedly. A few flares were fired from the SUGAR LOAF in N.8.d.

Much movement was observed throughout the day on the AUBERS-FROMELLES ROAD; also on RUE DELEVAL from N.14.b.80.25. to N.14.b.7.2. including two men carrying camp kettles in a N.E. direction. Several men were seen to enter   or leave the house at N.21.a.65.50. This house seems to be much used by parties coming in or out of IRMA C.T.

At 4.30 p.m. a party of about 20 Germans were seen at N.26.a.5.3. Smoke was seen at :-
```
        N.20.b.20.45.     MOSSY TRENCH
        N.21.d.2.1 )
               &   )      AUBERS DEFENCES.
        40.15      )
```

Head Qrs. 56th Divn.
29th January, 1917.

T.L.C.Hield
                                        Lieutenant,
                              Intelligence, General Staff.

56th DIVISIONAL TACTICAL PROGRESS REPORT No. 96.
from 8.0 a.m. 29th January to 3.0 a.m. 30th January, 1917.

On receipt of current copy of Divisional Tactical Progress Report in the trenches, previous copy to Bo destroyed.

PART I OPERATIONS.

RIGHT SECTION. Our trench mortars bombarded the enemy wire between M.36.a.35.95. and 35.80. with good effect, much wire being torn up and thrown into the air. The enemy retaliated with rifle grenades and as we still continued firing, the enemy opened with H.E. Later in the day we bombarded the enemy trench from M.30.c.30.49. to 60.45. with enfilade trench mortar fire with good results. The enemy again retaliated with H.E. and a few heavy trench mortars. Our machine guns carried out their usual night programme. Our patrols were out continuously throughout the night. Three enemy posts were located at M.36.a.40.70. - 37.50. - 35.30. our patrol being fired on from all three points. A machine gun fired from post at M.36.a.35.39. Another patrol located an enemy standing patrol of 14 men outside their trench, opposite M.29 / lewis guns opened fire on it. Another patrol entered the enemy line at M.30.a.50.05. and examined the trench to about M.30.a. - 40.15. Another patrol entered the enemy line at M.30.c.55.90. and proceeded towards his support line; a dugout was entered which had been very much knocked about. They heard movement in support line which was evidently occupied. Another patrol entered the enemy line at M.30.a.25.15. and proceeded along to M.30.a.50.20. The enemy's wire here was in good condition and the trench in a good state of repair. Another patrol approached the enemy front line at M.30.a.65.70., the wire was found to be quite good, largely knife rests and "gooseberries." no gap could be found, the trench there was occupied; talking and stamping of feet being heard and Very lights fired. Other patrols report enemy working party at M.24.d.50.15. where the wire had been repaired, enemy talking in front line opposite M.24.2. The enemy seems to be re-occupying this section of his front line, movement being reported here for the last three nights.

LEFT SECTION. During the day our artillery in co-operation with our heavy and medium trench mortars bombarded BERTHA C.T. and the river LAIES with good results. Our guns also fired on the house at N.25.b.8.9. and set it on fire. At 6.30 p.m. our artillery opened a sudden intense bombardment on (a) posts along the River LAIES in the region of BERTHA C.T. (b) junction of BERTHA C.T. and RUE DELEVAL (c) houses in LE PIETRE. The bombardment lasted six minutes and was very intense. Our machine guns fired heavy bursts down the tracks beside BERTHA Trench during and following this shoot. A patrol consisting of one N.C.O., 7 men and a Lewis gun and team entered the enemy line at N.13.d.60.55. The Lewis gun team was left there to cover the patrol's advance, the remainder proceeded towards the River LAIES crossed the old trenches at M.13.d.60.40. and reached the drain at N.13.d.60.32. This is about 20' wide. Patrol then fired two rifle grenades at N.19.b.40.95. which brought no retaliation. They then fired a Very light and a party of the enemy was seen at about N.19.b.35.80. The patrol opened rapid fire on them. The enemy divided into two parties one to the left and one to the right. They lay down and when the firing had ceased, commenced to advance as if to outflank the patrol. Each party estimated to be 20 strong. Our patrol withdrew to our Lewis Gun which opened fire and dispersed the enemy. The moon was very bright so shortly afterwards our patrol withdrew. Another patrol saw an enemy patrol between N.14.c.20.50. and 40.60. They opened rapid fire on them and dispersed them. Another of our parties which was cutting revetment wires between ENFIELD and RUE d'ENFER with a covering party protecting their right was attacked from the right by a strong party of the enemy. After a sharp scrap our party withdrew to our own lines. It was found that one of this party was missing so a search party went out and thoroughly searched the ground covered by the working party for nearly two hours with no result. A small patrol which went out at 3.40 a.m. with the object of leaving evidence of occupation in ENFIELD POST discovered a hostile party between them and the post. The enemy extended, so our patrol withdrew.

/ INTELLIGENCE.

PART II INTELLIGENCE.

RIGHT SECTION. Hostile artillery fired a few shells on to our C.Ts. without doing any damage. A few M.T.M. shells fell in the region of M.29.3. A hostile machine gun was firing from the enemy front line at M.30.a.50.05. A new brushwood screen has been erected in front of the small trench near GRETCHEN at N.23.b.05.65. Hostile aeroplane was reported to be ranging and calling up station "AU" at 11 a.m. At 2.45 p.m. a party of from 20 to 30 men was observed moving along the AUBERS - BAS POMMEREAU Road. Our artillery opened fire and they scattered towards AUBERS. Our howitzers bombarded the strong point at N.25.b.8.9. with incendiary shells and at dusk large clouds of smoke could be seen rising from the ruins at this point. Movement was observed from the enemy front line by KATHI C.T. Smoke was seen at M.36.c.07.60. and M.36.a.30.20. Two men were seen to enter the house in AUBERS at N.27.a.5.3.

LEFT SECTION. Hostile artillery was quiet except for shelling of our old posts in the German front line. A screen has been erected between N.25.b.7.8. and N.25.b.1.5. Movement was seen during the morning round the houses in LE PIETRE and 14 TREE CLUMP (N.20.b.-.45.40.) The tramway in N.21.a. was much used yesterday, but all the movement observed was in a S.E. direction. Odd parties of 2 or 3 men were seen on RUE DELEVAL between N.14.b.85.25. and 7.2. They all wore greatcoats and soft caps and carried rifles. At 4.0 p.m. two men each carrying a small box ran across the open from the wood at N.15.c.8.2. to IRMA C.T. This has been observed on several previous occasions and it is thought this wood is occupied. Usual movement and work was seen in the AUBERS Defences at N.21.d. A 4.2" hostile how. battery No. 149, was located by its flashes to be in action last night. Smoke was seen at N.20.b.30.40. house: N.20.b.25.50. head of MOSSY Trench; and N.20.d.90.85. house.

Hdqrs. 56th Divn.

30th January, 1917.

W.C.Heald

Lieutenant,

Intelligence, General Staff.

Appendix III

56th DIVISIONAL TACTICAL PROGRESS REPORT No. 87
from 8. 0 a.m. 30th January to 8. 0 a.m. 31st January 1917.

On receipt of current copy of Divisional Tactical Progress Report
in the trenches, previous copy to be destroyed.

PART I OPERATIONS.

LEFT SECTION.- Our artillery dispersed several working parties in the course of the day, whilst our T.Ms. fired on to enemy positions in N.14.a. Our machine guns carried out their usual night programme.
One of our patrols went out to investigate movement reported on parapet of old German front line at N.13.d.10.55. Patrol entered the German trench on the point of the WICK SALIENT but could find no signs of the enemy. They then proceeded to BARNET and ENFIELD POST and waited there 1 hour - no results. The going was extremely bad and the trench between BARNET POST and N.13.d.2.6. particularly damaged. Another patrol entered the German line at N.14.b.12.82. which they examined as far as the SUGAR LOAF, no enemy were seen or heard. They cut the wire holding the revetments for 50 yards.
Another patrol reconnoitred FLAME POST and cut revetting wire.
Another patrol proceeded to BERTHA POST. When they were about 16 yards away, they were fired upon, the post being occupied by the enemy. Two other patrols attempted to reach the post later but were all fired upon and forced to retire. The Post was bombarded with Stokes mortars.

RIGHT SECTION.- Our T.Ms. carried out a bombardment of the German trenches at the following points :- M.30.a.8.0. where movement had been observed, M.30.c.6.0. suspected trench mortar emplacement, and M.36.a.8.2. Much damage was caused at these points, many direct hits being obtained. Our patrols were very active last night, but for the most part saw no signs of the enemy. The German trenches were entered at the following points :- M.30.a.40.14., M.30.a.50.05., M.30.c.50.80. and M.30.a. central. No signs of occupation could be found in any of these points, though an enemy working party had been heard earlier in the evening about M.30.a. central. The wire in front of M.30.c.50.60. has been repaired by the enemy, and is now thick and strong. One of our patrols located a hostile party about 10 strong at M.30.a.50.65 moving in a Southerly direction. They were unable to approach it owing to the bright moon and snow.

PART II INTELLIGENCE.

LEFT SECTION.- Hostile artillery were fairly active during the day firing for the most part on to our C.Ts. Two machine guns were active during the night firing from points N.13.d.9.7. and N.13.c. 95.25. Considerable movement of small parties of men was seen during the day in rear of the German trenches, especially on the tracks in N.20.b.and N.21.a. The screens covering these tracks appear to have been much damaged by our recent artillery fire. All the men observed seemed exceptionally eager to avoid being seen and ran several hundreds of yards across the gaps. There was much movement around the dump at N.21.b.35.15. Our artillery dealt with this. Between 9 and 9.30 a.m. the heads and shoulders of one or two men could be seen over the low screen on RUE DELEVAL at N.14.b. 7.2. A man was seen to throw water out of the trench at N.14.d. 87.87. Much new work has been done recently on the wire in front of AUBERS DEFENCES from N.27.a. central to N.21.d. A new line of wire is being constructed, consisting of wire on 6 or 7 wooden stakes each about 3 yards apart, giving a total depth of about 20 yards. At present a large proportion of the stakes are without wire. The stakes are about 4 ftt high. A man was observed looking over the parapet in AUBERS DEFENCES at several points in N.21.d. Bertha C.T. in N.14.c. and N.20.a. has been much damaged by our shelling on the 29th. No signs of any new work are visible. Two conspicuous telegraph poles which for some time have marked the crossing of the railway over the AUBERS - FROMELLES ROAD have been removed by the enemy. The point at N.20.c.9.4. to which tracks lead from all directions, shown on Air Photo No. 10 A 716 was located today and seems to be a large fresh shell hole or possibly small pit. Fixed in the ground by the side of this is a

/notice

LEFT SECTION (contd.)

notice board about 10" by 6" on a stick 2 ft. high. This might be a M.G. position for night firing. A white tape is visible on the parapet at N.19.a.30.32, also on DORA C.T. from N.19.c.40.06 to enemy front line. There is a pioneer dump at N.25.b.80.95. Flares were sent up from the enemy post in front of TRIVELET.

Smoke was seen at N.19.c.70.18. ruins
    N.26.c.25.86.)
    N.20.a.95.65.) dugouts
    N.20.b.1.5.   )
    N.20.d.50.85.)
    N.21.a.97.50.

RIGHT SECTION. - Hostile artillery fired intermittently on to the area CHAPIGNY Fm. and GRANT'S Post M.23 and M.24.

Hostile T.Ms. were active during the afternoon and evening on MAUQUISSART CRATERS M.29.1. and M.35.4. A Minnewerfer was located at M.36.a.78.58. the gun crew being seen to leave the gun before each round was fired. Arrangements have been made to deal with this. A Machine Gun was firing from about M.30.c.8.8. The usual movement was observed in the MIN DU PIETRE. New work was observed along the road from N.25.c. to M.30.d.

Considerable movement was observed on the track from N.32.d. to N.33.c. including a party of 20 men each carrying a glittering flat object about 3 ft. by 1 ft. Usual movement was seen at tramway corner in N.26.c.8.3, and on the new trench in rear.

At 3.45 p.m. a hostile 77 mm. gun was located from M.23.d. 3.2. on a true bearing of 120° target RUE TILLELOY in N.13.a. The observer reported that the gun is close up and this side of EAS POMMEREAU and it is thought to be an enfilade gun in or near the house at N.31.b.8.6. Smoke was seen just in rear of the DISTILLERY CHIMNEY in N.19.c. also at many places in the German front line in M.36.a. and M.36.c. This portion of the trench has always been thickly manned.

Head Qrs. 56th Divn.
31st January, 1917.

Lieutenant,
Intelligence, General Staff.

FEB
1917

THE NATIONAL ARCHIVES (TNA): TERMS AND CONDITIONS FOR THE SUPPLY OF COPIES OF RECORDS

Copyright

1. Most public records in TNA are in Crown Copyright
There are no restrictions on the use of copies for non-commercial research or private study. Copies, and copies of those copies, may be made and used for education purposes. This covers both teaching and preparation for teaching and/or examination by either teacher or student. Applications for permission to use copies for publication (including web-site publication), exhibition or broadcast or any other purpose must be addressed to TNA Image Library, The National Archives, Kew, Richmond, Surrey TW9 4DU. Email: image-library@nationalarchives.gov.uk

2. Copies of Public Records in privately owned (ie not Crown) Copyright
There are no restrictions on the use of copies for non-commercial research, private study or education (as defined above) within the limits set in UK Copyright Law. Applications for permission to use copies for publication (including web-site publication), exhibition or broadcast or any other purpose must be addressed to the current owner(s) of the Copyright in the original document. Anyone wishing to reproduce the material in transcript, translation or facsimile is responsible for identifying the current owner and for obtaining any permission required. An application must also be made to TNA Image Library (address as above) for use of the copy.

3. Copies of non-public records and of published Copyright works held in TNA
These are supplied subject to the customer completing a declaration form and observing the conditions it contains. Any infringement of these conditions may result in legal action. Any use other than for non-commercial research, private study or education, if approved by the copyright owner, may also require the permission of the Image Library.
TNA Copyright Officer will provide further information on request.

Supplying copies

4. Prices quoted on estimates are valid for three months.

5. Orders for copies placed in person at one of TNA's Record Copying counters are accepted on the following conditions:
   a) TNA may cancel the order if the copying process paid for subsequently proves to be unsuitable, e.g. if it may damage the document or fail to produce good copies. If an order is cancelled for such reasons TNA will offer to refund the payment and if feasible will provide an estimate for completing the work by an alternative copying process.
   b) TNA may cancel the order and refund payments if markers are found to be missing, documents are incorrectly marked up, or customers' instructions are unclear.
   c) If the customer's calculation of the number of copies required proves to be an under-estimate TNA will complete the order but will retain the copies until the balance of payment has been received. If it proves to be an overestimate TNA will refund customers where the balance exceeds £3.00 (or £6.00 for overseas customers).

6. TNA will securely package copies supplied by post and will not accept liability in the event of damage or loss in transit. It can, however, arrange insurance cover at an additional cost if customers request it when they place their order. Such cover will usually be provided by a lower rate international recorded delivery unless otherwise requested by the customer.

7. Customers are advised to seek advise from their Internet Service Provider before placing any order for electronic images to be delivered electronically. Customers should note that digital images are supplied in compressed jpeg format via a link to TNA DocumentsOnline site unless specified otherwise and CD images in tif format. A0 images can only be requested on CD-ROM.

8. TNA will normally aim to provide 'research' quality copies, i.e. sufficient to convey written or graphic information in the original document. There can be no guarantee that it will be able to do so or that the copies will be suitable for any other purpose, e.g. if the original documents are of poor quality. Higher quality copies or copies suitable for other purposes can be supplied if requested when placing an order. Customers are advised to discuss their requirements with TNA staff to ensure the most suitable process can be recommended.

9. Image sizes:
   a) Photocopies and digitally scanned images: TNA will normally produce copied images, which are approximately the same size as the originals. Photocopies will normally be printed onto sheets of paper of the appropriate size in the A2 to A3 range (within preservation guidelines and at the discretion of the operator) and charges will be based on the size of the paper. In the case of digitally scanned copies the images will normally be printed onto paper approximately the same size as the original and charges will be based on the size category into which the paper falls (i.e. A0 to A1, A1 to A2, A2 to A3, A3 to A4. TNA can supply images of sheets of paper of different sizes if customers request it when they place their order.
   b) Prints from microfilm: images will normally be printed onto A3 size paper and may be larger or smaller than the original documents.
   c) Photographs or transparencies can be supplied in the specified dimensions. These will normally be required if a copy is for publication. The Image Library provides such images at the rates indicated in the appropriate leaflet.

Deemed Acceptance

10. TNA will display these terms and conditions at all points of sale. Customers will be deemed to have accepted the terms and conditions in completing an order form, submitting a counter order or accepting documents by any means.

RSDT drive\PSdev\PSDP\SSP self service copying\Terms and Conditions - 2.7.2003

YM/3

CONFIDENTIAL

War Diary

of

"G" Branch, 56th Division

from 1st February to 28th February 1917

(Volume XIII)

Army Form C. 2118.

WAR DIARY
or
INTELLIGENCE SUMMARY.
(Erase heading not required.)

Instructions regarding War Diaries and Intelligence Summaries are contained in F. S. Regs., Part II. and the Staff Manual respectively. Title pages will be prepared in manuscript.

Place	Date	Hour	Summary of Events and Information	Remarks and references to Appendices
La Gorgue	1st Feb		Quiet Period.	
	2nd		Enemy artillery activity on our centre section. Relief of 111 Bde by 168 Bde carried out without incident.	
	3rd		Artillery activity on both sides. Letter from the Corps Commander, showing his appreciation of the fine work done by the Division in the recent occupation of the German front line, received.	Appendix IV
	4th		Comparatively quiet day. Our patrols were very active at night. The German trenches were entered at a point much further South than ever before. Much useful information was obtained as to the position of enemy posts etc.	
	5th		Quiet day. Enemy used gas shells from T.M's last night. It is reoccupying his old front line in the left section. Frost still continuing.	
	6th		Quiet day. Some hostile artillery and T.M activity near NEUVE CHAPELLE. Our snipers killed several Germans during the day.	
	7th		167 and 169 Inf Brigades carried out inter-battalion reliefs without incident. 167 Bde made a dummy raid against the German trenches in M30c. They exploded a Bangalore torpedo in the enemy's wire, successfully destroying it. Enemy was slow in retaliating.	

WAR DIARY
or
INTELLIGENCE SUMMARY.
(Erase heading not required.)

Army Form C. 2118.

Instructions regarding War Diaries and Intelligence Summaries are contained in F. S. Regs., Part II. and the Staff Manual respectively. Title pages will be prepared in manuscript.

Place	Date	Hour	Summary of Events and Information	Remarks and references to Appendices
La Gorgue	8th Feb		168 Bde carried out an inter-battalion relief. Otherwise quiet day. Narration of the operations in the German lines Fauquissart Section - Compiled by XI Corps received & distributed	Appendix IV
	9th		Hostile raiding party entered our trenches after an intense bombardment at the point where the LA BASSEE Rd crosses our trenches. They were immediately attacked by the garrisons of the posts on either flank and driven out leaving two dead and one wounded (since died) in our trenches. Three belonged to the 13th Bav.I.R. (Normal)	Appendix
	10th		Two raids were carried out by 167 Inf Bde in the evening. In both cases the enemy's trenches were entered. Four Germans are known to have been killed & dugouts bombed by one party. The other party reached the German trenches on our two bomb barrels but did not find any of the enemy. Our casualties very slight. The enemy's trenches were in addition disturbed by artillery barrages. Quiet night afterwards	
	11		Quiet day. Enemy working hard on his old front line trenches in FAUQUISSART Section	
	12		Quiet day. Our patrols entered enemy trenches in several points in FAUQUISSART section & dispersed enemy parties there	
	13		168 Bde carried out a dummy raid on enemy line in M.35.d - no infantry action - with the object of discovering him as to the point of entry to the real raid to come	

Army Form C. 2118.

WAR DIARY
or
INTELLIGENCE SUMMARY.
(Erase heading not required.)

Place	Date	Hour	Summary of Events and Information	Remarks and references to Appendices
LAGORGUE	13th (contd)		One of our patrols after a short bombardment rushed an enemy post in No Mans Land from which the enemy had fled – 167 Bde carried out an internal relief	
	14th		Quiet day – Our patrols active and came into contact with the enemy at several points – 168 + 169 Bdes carried out internal relief	
	15th		Artillery activity on both sides – Much enemy work has been done in its regime to DEVILS JUMP in spite of our fire. Our patrols obtained contact with the enemy at several points in the region.	
	16th		A small raid was attempted by 3rd London Regt opposite MAUQUISSART enclosure, but the enemy were found alert and an entry could not be effected.	
	17th		A successful raid was carried out by the 13th LONDON Regt on the enemy lines – S.10.d. The parts penetrated both enemy lines + brought back 5 prisoners of the 13th Bavarian Regt besides killing a number, estimated at between 30 and 40 – The Chief of the Imperial General Staff visited the G.O.C. The G.O.C. + G.S.O.1 went to XVIII Corps H.Q.	
	18th		A raid was carried out by 5th LONDON Regt – The enemy trenches were entered at DEVILS JUMP + JUMP descended + and 1 officer and 1 or 2 HAMPSTEAD POST, in the three German were killed.	

Army Form C. 2118.

WAR DIARY
or
INTELLIGENCE SUMMARY.
(Erase heading not required.)

Instructions regarding War Diaries and Intelligence Summaries are contained in F.S. Regs., Part II. and the Staff Manual respectively. Title pages will be prepared in manuscript.

Place	Date	Hour	Summary of Events and Information	Remarks and references to Appendices
LA GORGUE	19th Feb.		An unusual amount of shell was carried at local garages, otherwise a quiet day. 167 and 169 Bdes carried on the battle relief.	
	20th Feb.		A quiet day. The enemy trenches were watched at several points found to be unoccupied. A hostile mine gallery was broken into opposite RED LAMP and destroyed. 168 Bde reliefs were carried out without incident.	
	22nd Feb		Enemy lines were shelled at several places again. Enemy lines were shelled at several places again. Situation quiet. Relief by 5th Div. of the 56th Div completed. XI Corps O.O. No 98 received giving arrangements for the movement of the 5th Div relieving the battle trenches (56 Div Warning Order No.6 issued) XI Corps D.O. No 101 giving details of relief received. XI Corps O.O. No 100 reference role of the Corps artillery.	APPENDIX I
	23rd Feb.		The usual patrol activity at night, but contact was not obtained with the enemy. 56 Div O.O. No 6a issued reference the extension of the divisional front owing to relief of XI Corps.	APPENDIX I

2353 Wt. W2544/7454 700,000 5/15 D.D.&L. A.D.S.S. Forms/C 2118.

Army Form C. 2118.

WAR DIARY
or
INTELLIGENCE SUMMARY.
(Erase heading not required.)

Instructions regarding War Diaries and Intelligence Summaries are contained in F. S. Rgs., Part II. and the Staff Manual respectively. Title pages will be prepared in manuscript.

Place	Date	Hour	Summary of Events and Information	Remarks and references to Appendices
LAGORGUE	24th Feb.		Hostile artillery + T.M were active all day.	
	25th Feb.		Hostile artillery was more active than usual along the whole front + our artillery replied vigorously. Fresh camps at the wood group Programme 51 Div. O.O. No.69 with details of the relief of the division carried	APPENDIX I
	26th Feb.		Reciprocal artillery activity during the period. Two 6" + one 8" batteries have been carrying out intensive registration of detail in his battery positions + on the open. 167 + 169 Bdes cooperated with enemy guns in unoccupied emplacements + from the open.	
	27th Feb.		Our artillery and T.Ms were active during the day, but failed to draw any considerable retaliation. 167 Bde carried out an extended relief.	
	28th Feb.		Hostile artillery was quiet but T.Ms active during the night.	

John T. Crofton Capr.
G.S. 5th DW.

SECRET.   Copy No 20

WARNING ORDER

56th DIVISIONAL ORDER No. 67.   February 22nd 1917.

The Division will be relieved by the 49th Division in the line between the 1st & 9th March.

2. General movements of the Division and the 49th Division between February 27th and March 11th are shewn on the attached Tables.

3. Guns will be exchanged between the 56th & 49th Divisional Artilleries.

During the transfer of the 49th Division to the First Army the guns will be parked at LUCHEUX until taken over by the 56th Divisional Artillery.

4. The Division will be accompanied by the Divisional Supply Column and Ammunition Sub-Park.

5. Detailed orders will follow later.

6. ACKNOWLEDGE.

Head Qrs. 56th Divn.   W.Brooks Captain
                                           Lieut-Colonel,
                                           General Staff.

Issued at 8.30pm

Copy No.				
1.	167th Infantry Brigade		13.	Sect. 15th Bty. M.M.G.Coy.
2.	168th Infantry Brigade		14.	56th Div.Signals.
3.	169th Infantry Brigade		15.	56th Div. Train.
4.	C.R.A.		16.	Div.Machine Gun Offr.
5.	C.R.E.		17.	257th Tunnelling Coy.
6 & 7.	XI Corps		18.	G.O.C.
8.	1/5th Cheshire Regiment		19.	A.D.C.
9.	A.D.M.S.		20.	War Diary.
10.	"Q"		21	File.
11.	A.P.M.		22.	New Zealand Divn.
12.	193rd Div. M.G.Coy.		23.	5th Division.
			24.	49th Division.

Attached to 56th Div. Order No.67.

MOVE of 49th DIVISION.

Serial No.	Unit.	Date.	From.	To.	
1.	A. Ede. Group 49th Divn.	1917 27th February	PERNES AREA	ST. VENANT AREA.	
	do.	28th February.	ST. VENANT AREA.	56th Div. Back Area.	
	do.	1/2nd March.	56th Div. Back Area.	Line in relief of 169th Inf.Ede./Group.	
2.	49th Div. less A & C Groups & less 2" T.M. Batteries.	3rd March.	PERNES AREA	ST. VENANT AREA	⎫ ⎬ Divisional ⎭ Artillery.
	do.	"	Divnl. Arty. LIGNY-les-AIRE	"	⎫ relieved by 49th ⎬ Divisional Arty.
	do.	4th March	ST. VENANT AREA.	56th Div. Back Area.	⎫ on the 4th, 5th ⎬ & 6th March.
	do	5/6th March.	56th Div. Back Area.	Line in relief of 167th Inf.Ede. Group.	

Attached to 58th Div. Order No.67.

MOVE of 49th DIVISION.

Serial No.	Unit.	Date. 1917.	From.	To.	
2.	49th Division, less A & B Groups, plus 2" T.M.Batteries.	7th March.	PERNES AREA.	ST. VENANT AREA.	
		8th March.	ST. VENANT.	56th Div. Back Area.	
		9/10th March.	56th Div. Back Area.	Line	in relief of 167th Inf.Bde.Groups.

MOVE of 56th DIVISION. Attached to 56th Div. Order No. ...

Serial No.	Unit.	Date.	From.	To.	
4.	169th Inf.Bde.Group.	1917. 1/2nd March.	Line.	56th Div. Back Area.	On relief by "A" Brigade Group, 49th Division.
	do.	2nd March.	56th Div. Back Area.	ST.VENANT AREA.	
	do.	3rd March.	ST.VENANT AREA.	PERNES AREA.	
5.	167th Inf.Bde.Group.	5/6th March.	Line.	56th Div. Back Area.	On relief by "B" Bde. Group 49th Division.
	do.	6th March.	56th Div. Back Area.	ST.VENANT AREA.	
	do.	7th March.	ST.VENANT AREA.	PERNES AREA.	
6.	56th Divisional Artillery.	6th March.	Line.	ST.VENANT AREA.	On relief by 49th Div. Arty.
		7th March.	ST.VENANT AREA.	LIGNY-les-AIRE	
		8th March.	LIGNY-les-AIRE.	Third Army.	
7.	168th Inf.Bde.Group plus Medium T.M.Batteries.	9/10th March.	Line.	56th Div. Back Area.	On relief by "C" Bde. Group 49th Division.
		10th March.	56th Div. back area.	ST.VENANT AREA.	If by Tactical Train the move from ST.VENANT will take place on the 10th - if by road on the 11th March.
		11th March.	ST.VENANT AREA.	PERNES AREA.	

War Diary

SECRET.

AMENDMENT TO WARNING ORDER No. 67.

With reference to 56th Divisional Order No. 67, dated February 22nd 1917, for " In relief of 167th Inf. Bde. Group" under Serial No. 3 of attached Move Order, read "In relief of 168th Inf. Bde. Group".

Head Qrs. 56th Divn.
23rd February, 1917.

[signed] Captain
Lieut-Colonel,
General Staff.

SECRET.   Copy No. .....

56th DIVISIONAL ORDER No. 68.

Reference Trench Map RICHEBOURG 1/10,000
"   Combined Sheet BETHUNE   1/40,000

23rd February, 1917.

Owing to a re-distribution of the Front between the 1st & XI Corps, the Boundary between the 56th & 5th Divisions will, on February 27th, be adjusted.

The new Boundary will run from CANADIAN ORCHARD (S.22.c.45.00) - S.27.a.60.85 - S.26.b.80.85 - S.25.b.70.35 - X.30.a.45.85 - X.21.a.20.40 - X.14.a.20.20 - W.11.a.60.00 thence along NORTH BANK of CANAL to P.36.a.80.70.

2. By 5 p.m. on the 27th February Brigade fronts will be adjusted as under:-

RIGHT BRIGADE.   S.22.c.45.00 to CHURCH ROAD (S.5.a.90.20) inclusive.

CENTRE BRIGADE. CHURCH ROAD (S.5.a.90.20) exclusive to WINCHESTER STREET (M.30.a.40.90) inclusive.

LEFT BRIGADE.   WINCHESTER STREET (M.30.a.40.90) exclusive to BOND STREET (N.8.d.90.00).

3. The following will be the Boundaries between

(a)   RIGHT & CENTRE BRIGADES.

S.5.a.90.20 - CHURCH ROAD - (exclusive to Centre Brigade) - L. & N. W. Ry. (inclusive to Centre Brigade) - M.26.a.80.70 - M.19.d.90.80 - R.23.b.80.20.

(b)   CENTRE & LEFT BRIGADES.

M.30.a.40.90 - WINCHESTER STREET (exclusive to Left Brigade) S. E. Ry. - EPINETTE DUMP (common to both Brigades) - M.16.a.60.50 - M.10.d.00.00 - M.10.a.10.50 - M.4.c.80.70 - M.1.d.20.30.

4. Posts to be taken and handed over in new Brigade areas are shewn on Map A.

5. All arrangements for the adjustment of Brigade fronts will be made between Brigadier Generals Commanding direct.

- 2 -

Headquarters of the Left Brigade of the 5th Division are at the/CENSE du RAUX (X.23.a.70.80).

6. The artillery of the 5th Division covering the new front to be taken over by the 168th Infantry Brigade - remain in position.

Further orders re the future dispositions of our artillery, on the withdrawal of the 5th Divisional Artillery, will be issued later.

7. Brigade Headquarters will remain in their present positions, with the exception that when signal communication is complete between the new Brigade Front of the 168th Brigade and the CENSE du RAUX, Headquarters 168th Infantry Brigade will move to the CENSE du RAUX.

8. Completion of moves to be notified to Divisional Headquarters.

9. ACKNOWLEDGE.

Headquarters 56th Divn.   W. Brooks Captain   Lieut-Colonel,
                                              for General Staff.

Issued at 2.30pm

Copy No. 1. 167th Inf. Bde.   15. Sec. 15th Bty.M.M.G.Coy.
         2. 168th Inf. Bde.   16. 56th Div. Signals.
         3. 169th Inf. Bde.   17. 56th Div. Train.
         4. 5th Division.   18. Divl. M.G. Officer.
         5. New Zealand Divn.   19. 257th Tunnelling Coy.
         6. C.R.A.   20. Divl. Gas Officer.
         7. C.R.E.   21. D.A.D.O.S.
     8 & 9. XI Corps.   22. 4th Aust. Div. Supply Col.
        10. 1/5th Cheshires.   23. No. 2 Amm. Sub-Park.
        11. A.D.M.S.   24. G.O.C.
        12. "Q".   25. A.D.C.
        13. A.P.M.   26. War Diary.
        14. 193rd Div.M.G.Cy.   27. File.

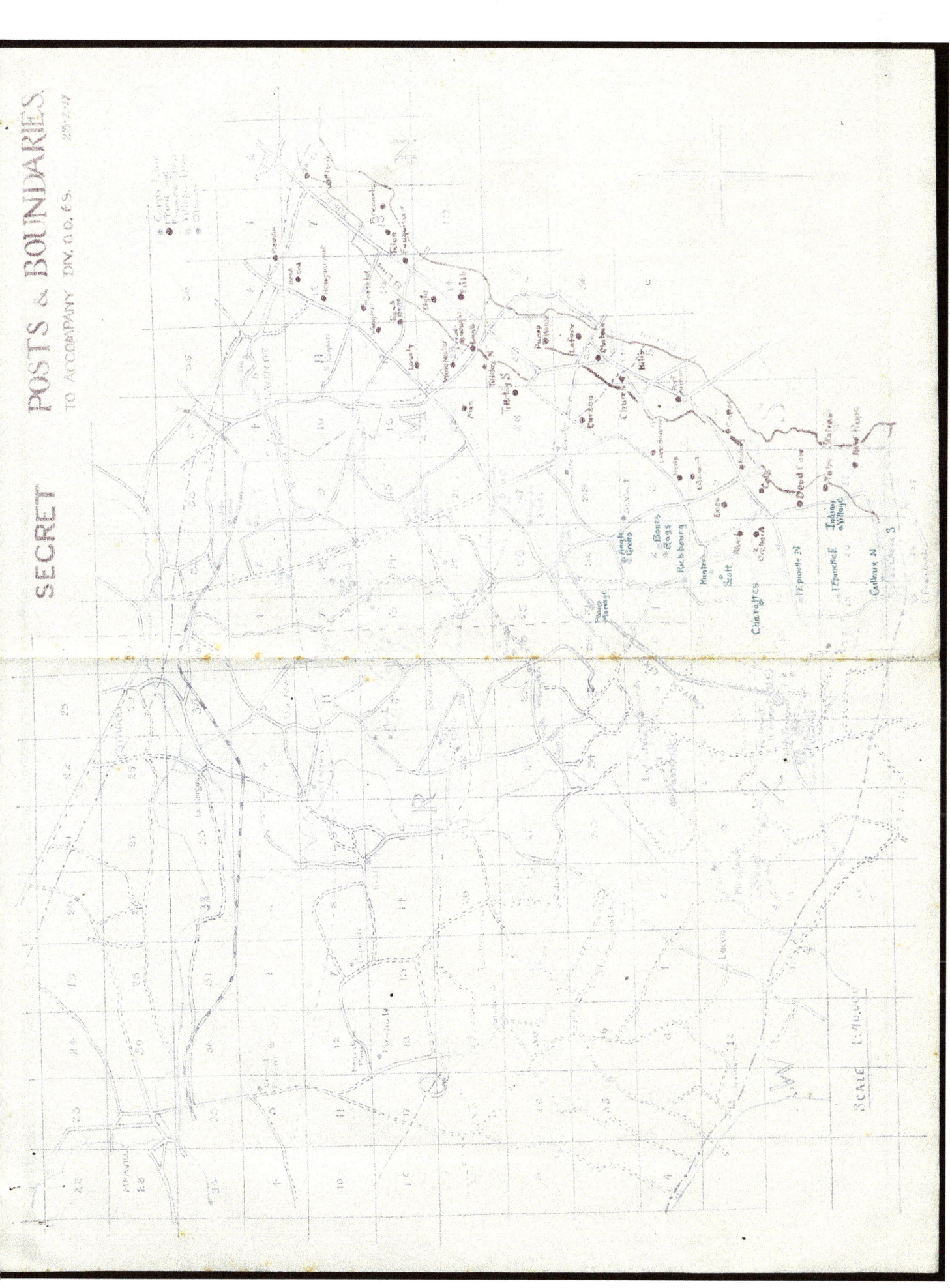

SECRET.   56th Division S.G.414/6

167th Inf. Bde.   Sec. 15th Bty. M.M.G.Coy.
168th Inf. Bde.   56th Div. Signals.
169th Inf. Bde.   56th Div. Train.
5th Division   Divnl. M.G.Officer.
New Zealand Divn.   257th Tunnelling Coy.
C.R.A.   Divnl. Gas Officer.
C.R.E.   D.A.D.O.S.
XI Corps.   4th Aust. Div. Supply Col.
1/5th Ches. Regt.   No. 2 Amm. Sub-Park.
A.D.M.S.   G.O.C.
"Q"   A.D.C.
A.P.M.   War Diary.
193rd Div. M.G.Coy.   File.

Reference 56th Division Order No. 68.-

1.   Guns of the 5th Division, at present covering the front to be taken over by the 56th Division, on the night February 27/28th i.e., CANADIAN ORCHARD (S.22.c.45.00.) to BOND STREET (S), will remain in position and will come under the orders of the G.O.C. 56th Division on completion of relief of this portion of the line.

2.   On relief of the 56th Division by 49th Division, guns of the 5th Division will continue in position covering the CANADIAN ORCHARD - BOND STREET front until further orders, and will come under the orders of the G.O.C., 49th Division on completion of the relief

3.   ACKNOWLEDGE.

Head Qrs. 56th Divn.
24th February, 1917.

                                        Captain
                                        Lieut-Colonel,
                                        General Staff.

SECRET

War Diary

56th Divn. S.G.415/7.

In continuation of 56th Div. Order No. 68 - EUSTON POST is inclusive to the CENTRE BRIGADE.

The Dump at M.27.d.7.3. is common to both the Left and Centre Brigades.

Head Qrs. 56th Divn.
25th February, 1917.

W.L. Brooker Captain,
Lieut-Colonel,
General Staff.

Copy No. 1. 167th Inf. Bde.
2. 168th Inf. Bde.
3. 169th Inf. Bde.
4. 5th Division.
5. New Zealand Div.
6. C.R.A.
7. C.R.E.
8 & 9. XI Corps
10. 1/5th Cheshire Regt.
11. A.D.M.S.
12. "Q"
13. A.P.M.
14. 193rd Div.M.G.Coy.
15. Sec.15th M.M.G.Coy.
16. 56th Div. Signals.
17. 56th Div. Train.
18. Divl. M.G.Officer.
19. 257th Tunnelling Coy.
20. Divl. Gas Officer.
21. D.A.D.O.S.
22. 4th Aust.Div.Supply Col.
23. No. 2 Amm. Sub Park.
24. G.O.C.
25. A.D.C.
26. War Diary.
27. File.

War Diary.

GENERAL STAFF
56th DIVISION.
No. SG 414/7/1

Reference 56th Divn. S.G.415/7 of 25.2.17, Dump at
M.27.d.7.3. for "common to Left & Centre Brigades" read "Right
& Centre Brigades"

John D. Crosthwaite Capt
for Lieut-Colonel,
General Staff.

Head Qrs. 56th Divn.
25th February, 1917.

Copy No. 1.   167th Inf. Bde.   15. Sec. 15th M.M.G.Coy.
      2.   168th Inf. Bde.   16. 56th Div. Signals.
      3.   169th Inf. Bde.   17. 56th Div. Train.
      4.   5th Division.   18. Divnl. M.G.Officer.
      5.   New Zealand Divn.   19. 257th Tunnelling Coy.
      6.   C.R.A.   20. Divl. Gas Officer.
      7.   C.R.E.   21. D.A.D.O.S.
   8.& 9.   XI Corps.   22. 4th Aust.Div.Supply Col.
    10.   1/5th Cheshire Regt.   23. No. 2 Amm. Sub Park.
    11.   A.D.M.S.   24. G.O.C.
    12.   "Q"   25. A.D.C.
    13.   A.P.M.   26. War Diary.
    14.   193rd Div. M.G.Coy.   27. File.

War Diary

SECRET.   Copy No. 30

56th DIVISION ORDER No. 69.

Ref. Maps - HAZEBROUCK, LENS SHEET 11, ABBEVILLE 1/100,000

25th February 1917

1. The Division will be relieved in the line by the 49th Division, and will be gradually transferred to the Third Army, where it will be administered by the XIX Corps.

2. The Division will be accompanied by its Divisional Supply Column and Ammunition Sub Park.

3. The Ammunition Sub Park will move without ammunition and be available for the carriage of blankets.

4. The 49th Division will leave their 18-pdr: guns and 4.5" Howitzers in the BOUBERS AREA. These guns and Howitzers will be taken over by the Division on arrival in the BOUBERS AREA.

5. The Medium Trench Mortars (and technical stores belonging to them) of the 49th Division will be taken over by the Division on the arrival of the last group in the WILLEMAN AREA.

6. The Division will move as shewn in the attached March Tables.

7. Accommodation Tables for PERNES & WILLEMAN also for ANVIN & BOUBERS Artillery Areas are attached.

8. Supply railheads will be notified later.

9. All reliefs will be arranged by Brigadier-Generals Commanding direct.

10. C.R.A's will arrange for the relief of the two Divisional Artilleries. The 56th Divn. will hand over all ammunition (including that in limbers) to the 49th Division.

11. C.R.E's will arrange for the relief of Head Qrs. R.E. Workshops, etc. The Field Companies will be relieved under orders of the Brigadier-Generals Commanding in whose Sectors they are working.

12. The A.D.M.S. will arrange for the relief of the Field Ambulances; Ambulances on completion of relief will join the Brigade Groups to which they are attached.

13. All defence schemes, sector maps, trench stores and aeroplane photos will be handed over and receipts taken.

14. The Command of the Left Sector of the XIth Corps Front will pass to the G.O.C., 49th Division on completion of relief.

15. Further orders will be issued concerning the move of Divisional H.Qrs.

16. ACKNOWLEDGE.

Head Qrs. 56th Divn.
  Issued at

Captain
for
Lieut-Colonel,
General Staff

P.T.O.

Copy No.	1. 167th Inf. Bde.	19.	Sec. 15th Bty. M.M.G.Coy.
	2. 168th Inf. Bde.	20.	56th Div. Signals.
	3. 169th Inf. Bde.	21.	56th Div. Train.
	4. 49th Division.	22.	Divl. M.G.Officer.
	5. XVIII Corps.	23.	257th Tunnelling Coy.
	6. XIX Corps.	24.	Divnl. Gas Officer.
	7. Third Army.	25.	D.A.D.O.S.
	8. 5th Division.	26.	4th Aust.Div.Supply Col.
	9. 57th Division.	27.	No. 2 Amm. Sub-Park.
	10. C.R.A.	28.	G.O.C.
	11. C.R.E.	29.	A.D.C.
12 & 13.	XI Corps.	30.	War Diary.
	14. 1/5th Ches. Regt.	31.	File.
	15. A.D.M.S.		
	16. "Q"		
	17. A.P.M.		
	18. 193rd Div.M.G.Coy.		

LOCATION TABLE FOR INFANTRY BRIGADES

	1	2	3	4	5	6	7	8	9	10	11	12	13	14	15	16	17	18	19	20	21	22
167th Infantry Brigade																						
Bde. H.Q.	Laventie (Cocksby House)																					
1st London Regt.	Pont du Hem																					
3rd " "	R	R	R	R	R	R	R	L	L	L	L	L	L	Riez Bailleul						Riez Bailleul		
7th Middlesex Regt.	Riez Bailleul							Pont du Hem						Pont du Hem								
8th " "	L	L	L	L	L	L	L	R	R	R	R	R	R	L	L	L	L	L	L	R	R	R
168th Infantry Brigade																						
Bde. H.Q.	Merville les Huit Maisons																					
4th London Regt. (Rangers)	Lagorgue Fosse						Croix Barbee		R	R	R	R	R	Croix Barbee						Fosse		
12th " " (Rangers)	Robermetz	L	L	L	L	L	L	R	L	L	L	L	L	L	L	L	L	L	L	L	L	L
13th " " (Kens.)	B.Dennis	R	R	R	R	R	R	L	R	R	R	R	R	R	R	R	R	R	R	Croix Barbee		
14th " " (Lond.Scot.)	Fr.Preaut Croix Barbee			Fosse																L	L	L
169th Infantry Brigade																						
Bde. H.Q.	Laventie — Roch sky Manor													Laventie & Rue Bacquerot						Laventie & Rue Bacquerot		
2nd London Regt. (R.F.)	Laventie						Laventie M.4.6.2.6.							Laventie						Laventie		
5th " " (L.R.B.)	R	R	R	R	R	R	R	R	R	R	R	R	R	R	R	R	R	R	R	L	L	L
9th " " (Q.V.R.)	L	L	L	L	L	L	L	L	L	L	L	L	L	L	L	L	L	L	L	Laventie		
16th " " (Q.W.R.)	Laventie & Rue Bacquerot						Laventie & Rue Bacquerot							Laventie						Laventie		
	R	R	R	R	R	R	R	R	R	R	R	R	R	R	R	R	R	R	R	R	R	R

NOTE:— Battalions in the trenches   RED
        Battalions in Support   BLACK

4.

		Billeting Accommodation.			Water Supply.	
		Offrs.	O.R.	Horses or Mules.	For Men.	For Horses.
No. 3 Bde. Area. Bde.H.Q.LE BOISLE.N.	CHEPIENNE. BERNAVILLE. LABROYE. LE BOISLE. * LE QUESNOY.	9 17 10 26 -	300 700 780 1600 -	50 - 214 200 -	5 wells. - Good wells. Pumps; plentiful supply. -	POND. - R. AUTHIE. R. AUTHIE. When allotted by G.H.Q.
		62.	3380.	464.		

GRAND TOTAL 303. 11510. 2625.
(exclusive of LE QUESNOY)

* Will be notified later.

Divisional Headquarters - WILLEMAN.

NOTE: The figures given are for normal easy billeting, with barns full. When the barns are empty, about 25% to 40% more men can be accommodated in the agricultural villages.

The figures for horses or mules are approximate only.

		Billeting Accommodation.		Horses or Mules:-	Water Supply. For men	For horses.
		Offrs.	O.R.			
No.1 Inf.Bde.Area. Bde.H.Q. OEUF.	NOULETTE. NOVELLE-les-HINNIERES.	8 4	300 300	- -	5 Wells. 5 Wells - indifferent water.	1 Pond - dry in summer. 1 Pond - dry in summer.
	FILLIEVRES.	42	1000	160	Wells - sufficient supply.	Ample - R. CANCHE.
	OEUF.	30	1500	400	Wells - do.	Insufficient locally: Springs at PRONAY - 4 mile Stream.
	WILLEMAN. FRESNOY.	20 12	550 300	250 30	50 Wells. 3 good wells.	Nil - Nearest supply R. CANCHE 1½ miles.
		116	3950	840.		
No.2 Bde.Area. Bde. H.Q. WAIL.	V:EIL HESDIN ST. GEORGES. WAIL. GALAMETZ VACQUERIETTE.	20 20 25 5 10	600 700 680 300 200	200 210 218 70 30	31 wells. Wells. 23 wells. 10 wells. 3 wells - 2 dry in summer.	R. CANCHE. R. CANCHE. R. CANCHE. R. CANCHE. Nil - Nearest supply R. CANCHE 2½ miles.
	ERQUIERES.	8	200	160	2 wells - 1 dry in summer.	8 Ponds - 6 dry in summer.
	QUOEUX. HAUTE MAISNIL. HARAVESNES.	11 10 2	500 200 200	50 187 70	3 wells. 4 wells. Wells - limited supply.	Pond dry in summer. 2 good ponds. Insufficient locally - R.CANCHE. 3 miles.
	FONTAINE L'ETALON.	14	600	126	Wells.	Sufficient for 126 horses.
		125	4180	1321.		

P. T. O.

War Diary

SECRET.   56th Divn. S.G.431/10.

AMENDMENTS & ADDITIONS to
56th DIV. ORDER No. 69, dated 25. 2. 17.

1. The 49th Divisional Artillery will relieve the 56th Divisional Artillery on the nights of March 4/5th & 5/6th - personnel of 4 guns of each Battery being relieved on the first night and 2 on the second night.

2. Reference 56th Div. Order No. 69, page 4, Serial No. 9, Column No. 6, for B.G.C. 168th Infantry Brigade Group, read B.G.C. 167th Infantry Brigade Group.

3. The Divisional Artillery will march from ST.VENANT - LIGNY-le-AIRE, via LILLERS & ST.HILAIRE.

John D. Crosthwaite Capt
Lieut-Colonel,
General Staff.

Head Qrs. 56th Divn.
28th February, 1917.

1. 167th Infantry Bde.
2. 168th Infantry Bde.
3. 169th Infantry Brigade
4. 49th Division.
5. XVIII Corps.
6. XIX Corps.
7. Third Army.
8. 5th Division.
9. 57th Division.
10. C.R.A.
11. C.R.E.
12.& 13. XI Corps.
14. 1/5th Ches. Regt.
15. A.D.M.S.
16. "Q"
17. A.P.M.
18. 193rd Div.M.G.Coy.
19. Sec.15th Bty.M.M.G.Coy.
20. 56th Div. Signals.
21. 56th Div. Train.
22. Divl.M.G.Officer
23. 257th Tunnelling Coy.
24. Divnl. Gas Officer
25. D.A.D.O.S.
26. 4th Aust.Div.Supply Col.
27. No. 2 Amm. Sub-Park.
28. G.O.C.
29. A.D.C.
30. War Diary.
31. File.

Location Table for Infantry Brigades

	FEBRUARY							MARCH															
	23	24	25	26	27	28	1	2	3	4	5	6	7	8	9	10	11	12	13	14	15	16
167th Infantry Brigade																						
Bde. H.Q.	Laventie		Cockshy House																			
1st. London Regt.	L	L	L	Pont du Hem																		
3rd. "	Riez Bailleul			R	R	R	R															
7th Middlesex Regt.	R	R	R	Riez Bailleul			L															
8th " "	Pont du Hem			L	L	L	L															
168th Infantry Brigade																						
Bde. H.Q.	Les Huit Maisons									Cense du Raux												
4th. London Regt.	R	R	R	Fosse			R															
12th " " (Rangers)	Fosse			R	R	R	R															
15th " " (Kens.)	Croix Barbee			L	L	L	L															
14th " " (Lond.Scot.)	L	L	L	Croix Barbee																		
169th Infantry Brigade																						
Bde. H.Q.	Laventie		M.4.b.2.c.				Lestrem - St Floris - Peynes - Willyman - No 3														
2nd London Regt. (R.F.)	L	L	Laventie				Lestrem No 1															
5th " " (L.R.B.)	Laventie			R	R	R	R			Vieille Chapelle												
9th " " (Q.V.R.)	Laventie			L	L	L	L			Lacouture No 2												
16th " " (Q.W.R.)	R	R	Rue Bacquerot				Boyt Boyle															

NOTE.—— Battalions in the trenches   RED.
        Battalions in Support   BLACK.

6.

FOURTH ARTILLERY AREA.

Divisional Artillery H.Q. - BOUBERS-SUR-CANCHE.

Note. - The figures are for normal easy billeting, when the barns are full. When the barns are empty, about 25 to 40% more men can be accommodated in the agricultural villages.

The figures for horses or mules under cover are approximate only.

	Billeting Accommodation.				Water Supply.	
	Offrs.	O.R.	Horses or Mules under cover.		Men.	Horses.
AUBROMETZ	15	500	250		Wells; supply sufficient.	Ample from River CANCHE.
MONCHEL.	7	450	100		" "	" " " "
CONCHY.	34	800	300		" "	" " " "
BOUBERS. *	30	600	350		" "	" " " "
TOTAL.	86	2350	1000			

* A Rest Station is established at BOUBERS.

ST. MICHEL, GROUCHES and ANVIN ARTILLERY AREAS.

Note :- The figures given are for normal easy billeting, with barns full. When the barns are empty, about 25% to 40% more men can be accommodated in the agricultural villages

The figures for horses or mules are approximate only.

Place.	Billeting Accommodation.			Water Supply.		Remarks.
	Offrs.	O.R.	Horses or Mules.	For Men.	For Horses.	
				St.MICHEL ARTILLERY AREA.		
St.MICHEL (including GRAND CAMP).	40	350	*	Wells.	Stream.	Standing Camp of 220 tents and 6 huts in addition. Accommodation in village is poor. * All horses of Divl. Arty. in open. Div. Arty. H.Q.St.MICHEL.
				GROUCHES ARTILLERY AREA.		
GROUCHES. & BOUT-DES-PRES. MILLY.	34 6 10	1000 200 350	401 170 570	Wells.	Stream.	Accommodation to complete to scale required for a Divl. Artillery is being provided by means of huts as material becomes available. of Divl. Arty. H.Q.
				ANVIN ARTILLERY AREA.		
HEUCHIN. BERGUENEUSE. ANVIN. MAISNIL LES TENEUR.	40 20 40 8	800 600 700 200	700 700 700 400	Pump and Well Wells. Stream. Wells.	Stream. Stream. Stream. Stream.	Divl. Arty. H.Q. 1 Bde. D.A.C., T.M.Btys. (part) 1 Bde. D.A.C., T.M.Btys. (part)
TOTAL:	108	2300	2500.			

56th DIVISION MARCH & RELIEF TABLE to accompany 56th DIV. ORDER No. 69.

Serial No.	Date. 1917.	Unit.	From.	To.	Route.	Remarks.
10.	March 3th	56th Div.Arty. (less Medium T.M.Batteries)	Line.	ST.VENANT AREA.		On relief by 49th Div. Artillery.
	" 7th	do.	ST.VENANT AREA	LIGNY-les-AIRE	No restrictions, under orders of the C.R.A. 56th Divn.	To be clear of ST. VENANT by 9 a.m.
	" 8th	do.	LIGNY-les-AIRE.	ANVIN Artillery Area.		Take over 18-pdr. guns & 4.5" Hows. left by 49th Division.
	" 9th	do.	ANVIN Artillery Area.	BOUBERS Artillery Area.		
11.	March 9/10th	168th Inf.Bde. Group, plus Medium T.Ms. except actual Mortars & technical stores belonging to Mortars.	Line,Right Section.	LA GORGUE - LESTREM, BOUT DEVILLE, VIEILLE CHAPELLE, etc.		On relief by 147th Inf. Bde. Group.
	March 10th or 11th.		FIRST ARMY AREA.	THIRD ARMY AREA.		If by Tactical Train on March 10th, if by Road on March 11th. Group will be accommodated in WILLEMAN AREA.No.1. Further orders will be issued.

56th DIVISION MARCH & RELIEF TABLE to accompany 56th DIV. ORDER No. 69.

Serial No.	Date 1917.	Unit.	From.	To.	Route.	Remarks.
6.	March 1/2nd	169th Inf.Bde. Group.	Line; Left Section.	LA GORGUE-LESTREM -BOUT DEVILLE - VIEILLE CHAPELLE.		On relief by 146th Inf. Bde. Group.
	March 2nd	do.	LA GORGUE - LESTREM -BOUT DEVILLE - VIEILLE CHAPELLE	ST.VENANT AREA	No restrictions, under orders of the B.G.C. 169th Inf.Bde.	(Units of Bde.Group will march at interval of 500 yards between Units. Not to enter LILLERS before 12 noon
	March 3rd	do.	ST.VENANT AREA.	PERNES AREA.		
	March 4th	do.	PERNES AREA	WILLEMAN No. 1 AREA.		
	March 5th	do.	WILLEMAN No. 1 AREA.	WILLEMAN No. 3 AREA.		
7.	March 4th	1/5th Ches. Regt.	LAVENTIE	MERVILLE - HAZEBROUCK RD. K.21. & K.22.		To be clear of LAVENTIE 12 noon.
	" 5th	do.	By bus to THIRD ARMY.			
8.	March 5/6th	167th Inf.Bde. Group.	Line- Centre Section.	LA GORGUE-LESTREM -BOUT DEVILLE - VIEILLE CHAPELLE.		On relief by 148th Inf.Bde.Group.
9.	March 6th	56th Division. (less 168th & 169th Inf. Bde.Group & Div.Arty.)	LA GORGUE - LESTREM -BOUT DEVILLE - VIEILLE CHAPELLE.	ST.VENANT AREA.	No restrictions, under orders of the B.G.C. 168th Inf.Bde.	Units of Brigade Group will march at intervals of 500 yds between Units.
	7th	do.	ST.VENANT AREA	PERNES AREA		
	8th	do.	PERNES AREA	WILLEMAN No. 2 AREA.		

p.2

49th DIVISION MARCH & RELIEF TABLE to accompany 56th Div. Order No. 69

Serial No.	Date 1917.	Unit.	From.	To.	Route.	Remarks.
4.	March 3rd	49th Div.Arty. (less Medium Trench Mortar Batteries)	LIGNY-les-AIRE.	ST.VENANT AREA.		
	March 4th, 5th & 6th.	Reconnaissance of the Line and Artillery Positions, relief of 56th Div. Artillery to be completed on the 6th.				
5.	March 8th	147th Inf.Bde. Group.	ST.VENANT AREA.	LA GORGUE, LESTREM, BOUT DEVILLE, VIEILLE CHAPELLE.		
	March 9/10th	do.	(LA GORGUE, LESTREM (BOUT DEVILLE, (VIEILLE CHAPELLE.	Line - Right Section.		In relief of 168th Inf. Bde. Group.

49th DIVISION MARCH & RELIEF TABLE to accompany 56th Div. Order No. 39.

Serial No.	Date. 1.17.	Unit.	From.	To.	Route.	Remarks.
1.	Feb. 27th	146th Inf.Bde. Group.	PERNES AREA	ST. VENANT AREA		
	Feb. 28th	do.	ST.VENANT AREA	LA GORGUE - LESTREM - BOUT DEVILLE -VIEILLE CHAPELLE, etc.		
	March 1/2nd	do.	LA GORGUE - LESTREM - BOUT DEVILLE - VIEILLE CHAPELLE.	Line - Left Section.		in relief of 169th Inf. Bde. Group.
2.	March 3rd	49th Div. H.Q. Section Signal Coy.	FIEFS	ST.VENANT AREA.		
	March 4th	49th Div. H.Q. Section Signal Coy.	ST.VENANT AREA	LESTREM.		
3.	March 3rd	148th Inf.Bde Group.	PERNES AREA.	ST.VENANT AREA.		
	March 4th	do.	ST.VENANT AREA	LA GORGUE - LESTREM - BOUT DEVILLE - VIEILLE CHAPELLE		
	March 5/6th	do.	LA GORGUE - LESTREM - BOUT DEVILLE - VIEILLE CHAPELLE.	Line - Centre Section.		in relief of 167th Inf. Bde. Group.

2.

	Billeting accommodation.			Water Supply.	
				For men.	For horses.
	Offrs	O.R.	Horses or Mules.		
No.3 Bde.Area. continued.					
ANTIN.	7	150	5	Wells.	Wells.
ANTIGNEUL	4	100	10	Wells.	Wells.
CHATEAU.	2	100	5	Wells.	Stream.
BRITEL.	4	100	200	3 wells.	Ponds.
GROSSART.	20	600	100	Pump and wells.	Ponds.
COUTEVILLE.	5	250	400	Wells.	Stream.
BETHONVAL.	7	150	—	Wells.	Stream.
BEIVAL.					
BOURS.					
CHARETU. }					
GRICOURT. }	35	1600	200	24 good wells.	Good stream.
NOZEILLES. }					
MORNEVILLE. }					
TOTAL.	625	15350	6600		

No.1 Inf.Bde.   225   4650   3180
No.2 Bde. Area. 252   5350   2200
No.3 Bde. Area. 148   5350   6600

PERNES AREA.
Divisional Headquarters - PERNES.

Note :- The figures given are for normal easy billeting, with barns full. Where barns are empty about 25 to 40% more men can be accommodated in the agricultural villages.

The figures for horses or mules are approximate only.

		Billeting accommodation			Water Supply.	
		Offrs.	O.R.	Horses or Mules.	For Men.	For Horses.
No.1 Inf.Bde.Area. Bde. H.Q. SACHIN.	FIEFS.	30	700	200	Wells.	Wells.
	BAILLEUL-les-PERNES.	25	450	500	Well.	Pond and Stream.
	AUMERVAL.	20	200	30	Well.	
	CAUCHY à la TOUR	70	1500	500	WELLS.	4 pools.
	FLORINGHEM.	30	700	1000	Wells - water not very good.	Wells - water not very good.
	SACHIN.	20	300	500	Wells - water not very good.	R. LA CLARENCE.
	BOYAVAL.	20	400	350	Pump and wells.	Pond.
	SAINS-les-PERNES.	10	400	100	Wells.	Pond.
No.2 Bde.Area. Bde. I.Q. PERNES.	PERNES.	130	2000	500	Tanks.	Pond and stream.
	BRESSY-les-PERNES & FAUX.	17	650	100	Wells.	Ponds.
	TANGRY.	30	800	200	Wells.	Pond.
	GUERNOUVAL and HESTRUS.	25	400	100	Pump and wells.	Ponds.
	EPS and HERBEVAL.	20	400	300	Pump and wells.	Stream.
	MORCHY CAYEUX.	30	1100	1000	Stream.	Stream.
No.3 Bde.Area. Bde. I.Q. ANTINEUL CHATEAU.	MAREST. VALHUON & LE HAMEL.	20	800	100	23 wells.	Stream.
		44	1500	200	Wells.	Wells.

P.T.O./

The following constitute BRIGADE GROUPS.

167th BRIGADE GROUP.

Head Qrs.	167th Infantry Brigade
	167th Infantry Brigade
	167th M.G.Coy.
	167th T.M.Battery
	416th Field Coy. R.E.
	No. 2 Coy. 56th Div. Train.
	2/1st Field Ambulance.

168th BRIGADE GROUP.

Head Qrs.	168th Infantry Brigade
	168th Infantry Brigade
	168th M.G.Coy.
	168th T.M.Battery.
	513th Field Coy. R.E.
	No. 3 Coy. 56th Div. Train.
	2/2nd Field Ambulance.

169th BRIGADE GROUP.

Head Qrs.	169th Infantry Brigade
	169th Infantry Brigade
	169th M.G.Coy.
	169th T.M.Battery.
	512th Field Coy. R.E.
	No. 4 Coy. 56th Div. Train.
	2/3rd Field Ambulance.

www.ingramcontent.com/pod-product-compliance
Lightning Source LLC
Chambersburg PA
CBHW081433160426
43193CB00013B/2272